Prima's Official Strategy Guide

Rick Barba

Prima Games
A Division of
Prima Communications, Inc.

3000 Lava Ridge Court
Roseville, CA 95661
(916) 787-7000
www.primagames.com

Project Editor: Jill Hinckley
Product Managers: Jennifer Crotteau, Michelle Medley

ISBN: 7615-2339-1

Library of Congress Catalog Card Number: 99-65504

Printed in the United States of America

00 01 02 03 BB 10 9 8 7 6 5

Table of Contents

1: CHEATS AND QUICK START TIPS 1
Cheat Codes 2
Quick Start Tips 6

2: PERSONALITY 10
How Personality Affects Sim Behavior 11
How Personality Affects Fun 16
How Personality Affects Skill Building 17
Sim Zodiac Signs 18

3: MOOD AND MOTIVES 19
The Motive Engine 20
How Mood Is Calculated 20
A Sim's Eight Basic Needs 23
Hunger: The Food Chain Revealed 24
Comfort 32
Hygiene and Bladder 33
Fun 34
Energy 35
Social 36
Room 37
Motive Failure States 41
Death 42

4: SIM AUTONOMY 45
A Note About the Queue 46
Advertising 47
Ad Modifiers 48
Exit Conditions 53
Object Advertising Table 56

5: SOCIAL INTERACTIONS 72
The Relationship Score 73
Influence of Mood and Personality 74
Topics of Conversation 74
Social Outcomes 81
How Social Interactions Are Scored 85
Friendship 88
The Romance Bit 89
Family and Housemates 91

Visitors 95
Ghosts! 101

6: CAREERS AND SKILLS 103
Careers 104
Skill Building 110
The 10 Career Tracks 112
School8 118

7: SIM ECONOMICS 101 120
Net Worth 122
Object Depreciation 122
Build Depreciation 128
Bills and the Repo Man 129
Services 131
Fire, Theft, and Accidents 135

8: BUILDING 139
A Special Note on Remodeling 141
Architecture Items 141
Terrain Tools 143
Plant Tool 144
Wall Tool 145
Floor Tool 147
Wallpaper Tool 147
Doors and Windows 148
Water Tool (Swimming Pool) 149
Stairs 150
Second Story 150

9: SIM OBJECTS 151
How Sims Appraise New Purchases 152
Repairing Broken Objects 153
Buy Mode 153
List of Object Interactions 154

10: CREATING YOUR OWN SIM STUFF 169
Where to Find New Sim Stuff 170
Make Your Own Stuff: Getting Started 171
FaceLift: How to Create Custom Sim Faces 173
HomeCrafter: How to Create Wall
and Floor Tiles 174
SimShow: How to Create Your Own Skins 175

Foreword

ntelligence is an interesting thing. It's a fairly recent innovation in evolution, our ancestors having basically been pond scum for about 3 billion years beforehand. The ability to adapt more rapidly (than genetic evolution) to changing environments seems to be the basic reward of intelligence. The cost of this intelligence is balanced against many other factors, from rate of reproduction (rabbits) to body mass (birds).

But why did humans go so overboard? Our brains are almost too big at birth, our young are not self-sufficient for years, and we're physically not that impressive compared to many other animals.

There seems to be some evidence that our intelligence is the result of a vicious feedback cycle, a cycle that begins with social behavior. At some point in our history we began to compensate for our weaknesses by banding together in tribes and clans, much like wild primates. Our family structures became more stable. The social structures in these groups—and our ancestor's individual standing within them—became a larger and larger component of our environment over time. Basically our roles and behaviors in these societies started to become as complex as the rest of the outside world.

Perhaps, it is thought, this became a major impetus for the growth of our brain mass. We needed bigger brains to be successful in our own societies (which were helping us to become successful at the game of survival). We needed to understand clearly the needs, motivations, and intentions of our families, clan members, and competing humanoids. Most of the other high intelligence animals on Earth also seem to be highly social creatures (dolphins, chimpanzees).

As our intelligence progressed, we evolved and devised ever more elaborate means of communication, culminating in the development of symbolic grammars like math, language, and music. From the perspective of other species on Earth we are almost telepathic in our abilities to communicate complex ideas to one another.

Along our path we came up with many interesting tools that allowed us to not only shape our external world of wood, rocks and fire, but also our internal world of communication, planning, and symbols. One of these tools was the game. Many animals exhibit the more general aspects of play (as a learning mechanism, where they can experiment with survival strategies while young), but only humans have taken play into the purely symbolic realm of games (with well-defined rules and metaphors).

So it seems only appropriate (and somewhat ironic) that the reason we are so tuned into the thoughts, feelings and motivations of other people is because that is what has been growing our brains for the last million years or so. We have become so adept at modeling the mental state of others because our societies (and hence survival) depended on that ability.

Seems like a good excuse for a rather odd game, anyway.

—Will Wright

Introduction

In January of 2000 we braved the Y2K skies and sojourned to Walnut Creek, California for a privileged tour of *The Sims* conducted by none other than Will Wright himself. Indeed, over the course of our three-day visit, Will graciously lifted the lid of his software "dollhouse" (the original working title of the game) and shared its inner secrets with us.

Now we pass them on to you.

And that's the beauty of an official strategy guide, isn't it? The words go directly from the design gods into our tape recorder, then onto the page, and then to you. So here, in your hands right now, you hold an intimate map to all of the secret places in *The Sims* that only Will Wright and his EA/Maxis team of developers knew about until they spilled the beans onto our hungry little micro-cassette recorder.

Before we proceed, however, let us make one very important point: *This strategy guide begins where The Sims game manual ends.* In fact, we assume you've not only read the excellent manual but have played the game a bit and have a basic familiarity with its controls. If you have not explored the manual yet, please do so now. It's a pleasant read filled with indispensable information about navigating *The Sims.*

That said, this guide is structured to have something for every type of Sim fan. Each chapter features a comprehensive examination of the inner workings of *The Sims,* peering into the very depths of the engine programming in many cases. But that shouldn't scare off casual gamers. Each section builds from a general strategy overview and includes plenty of simple, straightforward tips in easy-to-find hint boxes.

Again, many of these tips come courtesy of the Maxis development team, including Will Wright himself, as do the dozens of point tables, graphs, charts, and other valuable game data you'll find in this book. Other nuggets of insight come from the *real* experts—the Electronic Arts testing team that crunched the game, day and night, for months on end. You'll find these gems in our "Tips from the Testers" sections liberally sprinkled throughout each chapter.

One last note: Be sure to check out the last section, "Creating Your Own Sim Stuff". It's remarkably easy to customize *The Sims* to model your own personal view of neighborhood life, no matter how unique or, OK, we'll say it, *perverse.* And take regular visits to the *The Sims* official website at http://www.thesims.com to "shop" for new catalog items for the game. (It's free, of course.)

Acknowledgments

The first thanks go to the obvious. Everybody, say it with me: *Thank you, Mr. Will.* My thanks go to Will Wright not only for the brilliant, addictive, non-violent game-of-the-year but for his generous help and warm hospitality during my visit to Maxis.

Second, this book would not have been remotely possible without the attentive oversight of Chris Trottier, associate producer for *The Sims*. Her patient review of early drafts and our daily e-mail exchanges kept things accurate and on track. Thanks also to software engineer Patrick J. Barrett III, who clarified and verified much of the information in this book, and to artist Eric Chin for providing graphic materials with amazing alacrity.

Last but not least, my deepest gratitude goes to the Electronic Arts testers who provided a wealth of helpful materials. Thanks to Andrew Blomquist, Syruss Flyte, Peter Trice, Ed O'Tey, and Jason Morales for their insightful tips (including the weird sadistic ones).

1
Cheats and Quick Start Tips

L et's kick off our pre-game coverage with the inside scoop, the real reason you bought this strategy guide in the first place (admit it)—cheat codes. We managed to scam a comprehensive list of codes from the Maxis development team.

We also strong-armed the Electronic Arts quality-control testers into revealing a few of their sneaky "quick-start" tips—clever ways to maximize your bank account in the early going.

Oh, and we found that the game's only known Easter egg (as of this writing) is the product of programmer Patrick Barrett, who broke down and revealed it to us after a couple of minor stalking incidents: after you use the Help System in *The Sims* for 100 days, it begins to give you info about design team members.

Thanks, Patrick. We'll be in touch.

Cheat Codes

To bring up the Cheat window, press Ctrl Shift C. Then key in the cheat code. Some cheat functions may seem arcane to the average player. Don't worry, they made us feel stupid, too. But hackers will probably find some useful tools for evading the NORAD detection 'bots.

water_tool

This cheat enables the water tool for landscaping your lot with water. To deactivate the water tool, go into Build mode and pick another tool. Hold down Ctrl and use the left mouse button to recreate land. Remember that water blocks Sims routing.

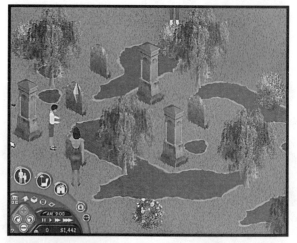

Fig. 1-1. Add streams, ponds, and creepy bogs (like this one, in the Goths' backyard cemetery) with the water tool cheat.

draw_routes (on/off)

Draw colored dots on the selected Sim's path. This one's kind of cool.

autonomy (0 to 100)

This cheat sets the autonomous behavior level of all the Sims in the house. Enter 0 to turn autonomy off, 50 to set it to normal level. Enter 100 for "super autonomy," which allows Sims to do things that only the users can do.

bubble_tweak (0 to -65)

This cheat sets the 'z' value to offset the Sims' thought bubbles. The default is -65, so the bubbles don't poke through the headboards on beds.

draw_all_frames (on/off)

Draw all animation frames without skipping to keep up. This allows you to view all animations but forces the game speed to zero at times.

draw_floorable (on/off)

Turns the floorable grid on and off in Build mode when you add a second story. It's defaulted to "on." ("Floorable" describes an area where you can place floor grids. Don't you love designer-speak?)

genable (various settings)

Use this cheat to turn the drawing of surfaces to screen on and off. We're not sure why anyone would *want* to turn stuff off, but here's the list:

genable default: Sets everything to default.

genable status: Shows current settings.

genable terrain (on/off): Enables/disables terrain drawing.

genable floors (on/off): Enables/disables floor drawing.

genable walls (on/off): Enables/disables wall drawing.

genable objects (on/off): Enables/disables object drawing.

genable people (on/off): Enables/disables people drawing.

genable all (on/off): Enables/disables all the foregoing.

grid (on/off)

Enables/disables terrain grid drawing.

grow_grass (amount)

Increases the grass level to the maximum for each tile. To turn brown grass to green on your lot, key in 150 as the amount.

history (file)

Writes the current family's history to a file. If the file is unspecified, the default is used. The default is FamilyHistory.txt, written to the Sims folder.

map_edit (on/off)

Use this cheat to lock and unlock floor tiles. You can't edit—that is, move objects, change terrain, build floors or walls, and so on—a locked tile. Such tiles usually lie at the edges of a lot. The mailbox and outside trash can lie on locked tiles, for example, as do the road and the border around the lot.

move_objects (on/off)

Turn this function on to move any object.

preview_anims (on/off)

Turns Animation Preview mode on and off. This function allows you to click on an object and view any selected Sim's animation for it. Why is this useful? It's a secret. Nobody can tell you.

rotation (0)

Sets a lot's rotation to its default, as seen from the Neighborhood screen.

route_balloons (on/off)

Defaulted off. Use this cheat to view a Sim's intermediate route balloon info.

set_hour (hour)

Set the time of day (hours 0 to 23).

sim_speed (speed)

This cheat alters the speed of the game. The range is from -1000 (a virtual crawl—kind of cool, like slo-mo) to 1000 (same as the Ultra Speed button on the Control Panel).

sim_log (begin/end)

Start and stop Sim logging. Writes a SimLog.txt file to the Sims folder.

Will Wright explains: "If you type 'sim_log begin' and play a while, the game will keep track of everything each character does. Typing 'sim_log end' stops and displays the text file.

"The file is a Tab-delimited text file that can easily be read into *Microsoft Excel*. The file includes a row of data for each interaction that's occurred, sorted by the object involved. This data includes routing time, interaction time, the change in each motive during interaction, and the character performing the interaction.

"We used this feature quite a lot during game tuning. I'm sure our players will figure out some really interesting things to do with this."

sweep (on/off/none)

Displays the in-game frame profiler. Click in the Sweep window and use your up/down arrow keys to change events being profiled, and your left/right arrow keys to adjust the milliseconds per tick.

You'll find this utility useful for running background checks on suspected Algerian terrorists, for example…

tile_info (on/off)

Show or hide the Tile Info window: move the mouse over a tile, click in the Tile Info window, and then press R to view base object info.

Quick Start Tips

We harassed EA testers Flyte and Blomquist into revealing the Fraternity of Testers' most intimate secrets for building cash quickly in *The Sims*. Here are a few of the more effective (and nefarious) tactics.

The Bob and Betty Cheat

If you've played the tutorial, you know Bob and Betty Newbie. This delightful couple provides a nice, safe introduction to *The Sims* because (as we learned by snooping through Will Wright's desk) the game's Motive engine mutes the usual degradation of their needs until you complete the tutorial.

Fig. 1-2. THE SIMS' tutorial, starring Bob and Betty Newbie, gives you sneaky, cheatin' ways to build a nest egg quickly.

In other words, neither Bob's nor Betty's needs drop very fast while the tutorial is active. Most, in fact, won't drop at all.

So here's a tip from Syruss Flyte, an Electronic Arts tester for *The Sims*: After Betty Newbie appears, ignore the tutorial directions for a while. Instead, get jobs for the Newbies, buy the espresso machine, put the game on Ultra Speed, and focus entirely on raising Bob's and Betty's skills.

The Hunger motive is frozen, so they won't need to eat. And, although they'll lose Energy at work and while exercising to increase their Body skill, they can recover by using the espresso machine five or six times instead of sleeping.

"In a relatively short time, Bob and Betty can max out all six of their skills," Flyte says.

After that, the super-Newbies move with alacrity up the ladder of success as they make more friends.

EA tester Andrew Blomquist adds, "After you get jobs for Bob and Betty and build up all their skills, just let the game run on Ultra Speed. Walk away. In fact, let it sit overnight. In the morning your Newbies will be stinking rich."

Then you can finish the tutorial, create your own Sim family, kill off either Bob or Betty, and have one of your own Sims marry the surviving Newbie.

"If you're feeling particularly cold-blooded," adds Blomquist, "kill off the Newbie you married and keep the money for your Sim widow or widower."

But remember, one of these maxed-out Newbies can be the workhorse of your family, getting quick promotions with big paychecks, and bonuses, and other good stuff.

As you can see, game testers are Machiavellian. Of course, you'd be amoral, too, if you spent all day chained in a dark pit.

Fig. 1-3. Here's the ultimate Newbie skill-building room—piano (Creativity), bookshelf (Cooking and Mechanical), mirror (Charisma), chessboard (Logic), and exercise machine (Body). Use the espresso machine on the desk to replenish Energy.

TIP

In *The Sims*, the houses are the saved games. Whenever you quit or return to the Neighborhood screen, you can save the changes to the house and its inhabitants. If you don't like the chain of events since you last saved, choose not to save, and then reenter the house from the Neighborhood screen.

The Slave Labor Method

Low-level jobs don't pay well, but it's the only employment you can find early in the game. The more workers you have bringing home paychecks at that time, the better.

Andrew Blomquist suggests you start a full-house "family" of eight Sim adults with the bare essentials for survival. Start seven Sims working right away and keep one poor slob home to keep house. Focus on the key survival motives—Hunger and Energy—but keep at least three of your folks in a good enough mood to advance their careers.

"You can just kill off the extra workers later," Blomquist adds coldly, "when the careers of your primary Sims stabilize and you have the equipment you need to get their motives up quickly and work on skills."

Fellow tester Syruss Flyte takes a slightly different approach to this method. Again, he suggests starting a family of eight Sim adults and putting them on an empty lot. Don't build anything, just place a good refrigerator. Then get each Sim a job. The best way to do this is to buy a cheap desk, computer, and chair. (Otherwise they all fight over the newspaper.)

Fig. 1-4. Meet the Slave Labor family. Launch careers for seven of these poor automatons and leave one at home to handle minimal housekeeping and cooking duties. Soon your bankbook swells...

Now run in Ultra Speed. This can be tricky. Your Sims will develop foul moods and fall asleep on the ground, so you have to make sure they go to work each day.

"But no matter how bad a mood your Sims develop, they never lose their jobs as long as you get them to their car pool," says Flyte. "With eight Sims working, you'll earn between §800 and §2,000 a day and, with only a fridge on the lot, the bills will be *very* low. Doesn't take long to build up a sizeable bank account."

You've got to admire the way Syruss thinks.

Marriage for Fun and Profit

This truly underhanded trick also comes courtesy of Syruss Flyte:

Create your family and move them onto a lot, but don't give them jobs. (Believe me, they won't have time to work with all the wooing that lies ahead.) Next, create a bunch of one-Sim "families," maxing out each Sim's personality with Nice and Outgoing points. Then move one of these single-Sim families into each remaining empty lot in the neighborhood. Give each lone Sim a small end table, a phone—and absolutely nothing else. Return to your family.

Now your family's entire focus is to meet, greet, befriend, flirt, and eventually marry every one of the lone Sim neighbors on the block. (Or, if the neighbors are the same sex, to convince them to join your household.)

Sure, you'll leave a trail of jealousy and broken hearts. But the payoff is big. Remember, whenever you marry the last adult Sim from another household, you gain not only a mate but also his or her entire net worth. In this case, each consummation brings your family almost $20,000 a pop. That adds up to a *lot* of simoleans.

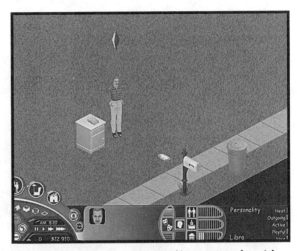

Fig. 1-5. Put one nice, outgoing Sim on every lot with just a cheap end table and a phone. (We named this guy Rich Wedbait. Get it? Get it?) Return to your household, and then have your family meet, woo, and marry all these affable Sims to get their assets.

The Big Box Method

Here's one last (and somewhat less extreme) startup trick from tester Andrew Blomquist. He suggests you can save a lot of money by not building interior walls at first.

"Walls cost money," he says, "and they increase the time it takes to route between objects." Indeed, walls are truly necessary only for bathroom privacy and to keep disturbances from awakening your sleeping Sims.

Blomquist says the best tactic is to build a simple one-by-two-tile room for both toilet and telephone. This gives you bathroom privacy and muffles the ringing phone. With the money you save, you can buy better objects for your Sims until money is no longer an issue.

2
Personality

hen you first jumped into *The Sims,* you probably moved one of the game's premade families into the neighborhood. (If you're a guy, admit it—you went for the Roomies.) Then, of course, you got the itch to create your own Sims. When you create your own Sim family, you select their heads, bodies, and—wonder of wonders—their *personality traits.*

In this section, we examine how personality traits affect Sim behavior. We also look at some the various preconfigured personality types—the zodiac signs—and see how they get along (or don't).

How Personality Affects Sim Behavior

When you construct a Sim, you assign points to five personality traits—Neat, Outgoing, Active, Playful, and Nice—in the Create a Sim screen. Changing the totals for these traits changes your Sim's attraction to certain activities and to other Sim types. For example, as the manual notes, a playful Sim is more likely to be drawn to pinball machine than to a bookshelf.

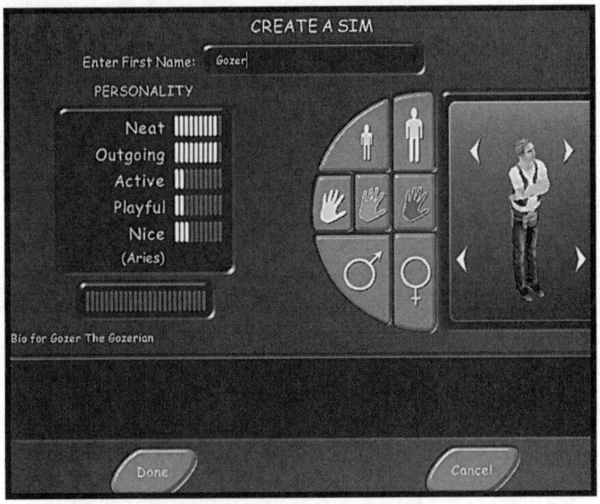

Assigning points from 0 to 10 for each trait is like moving a slider bar between opposites. At 0 points, your Sim actually manifests the *opposite* of a particular trait. Thus, there are really 10 personality traits in *The Sims,* set up as pairs of opposites. They are:

Neat/Messy

Outgoing/Shy

Active/Lazy

Playful/Serious

Nice/Grouchy

Fig. 2-1. Each personality trait encompasses both itself and its opposite. Here, Gozer is high on Neat and Outgoing, but is Lazy (low Active), Serious (low Playful), and Grouchy (low Nice).

Smooth-running Sim households often mix Sims with different traits for an efficient division of labor—a neatnik housekeeper, a nice and outgoing friend-maker, and so forth. Let's take a look at the activities associated with each personality trait.

Tips from the Testers

Choose your personalities to fit the roles you want your Sims to play. Neat Sims make very good stay-at-home cleaners. Outgoing and Nice helps a Sim looking to make family friends. Playful makes the Entertain and Joke interactions more readily available. Active Sims keep on the go and don't get uncomfortable easily.

—Peter Trice, Tester

Neat/Messy

Cleaning activities reach out and grab neat Sims. Neatniks are more likely to autonomously empty the trash, sweep up ash, mop up spills, clean up after meals, make

Fig. 2-2. Sims with high Neat points make swell stay-at-home housekeepers.

beds, water flowers, bathe, wash hands, brush teeth, flush and clean toilets, clean tubs and showers, wind the old grandfather clock, and turn off the computer.

In fact, the following actions "push" to the front of the queue, based on your Sim's Neat rating. (For more on this, see the "Push" section in "Sim Autonomy" later in the book.)

On their own, neat Sims will:

- Wash their hands after eating pizza
- Flush and wash their hands after using the toilet
- Wash their hands after cleaning the toilet
- Make the bed after waking up

Messy Sims will:

- Create a puddle when getting out of the shower or bathtub
- Create a puddle when cleaning the aquarium
- Throw trash on the floor after eating a snack
- Leave a dirty plate after a meal

Outgoing/Shy

Outgoing Sims are people who need people. The Social motive score drops faster for them, so they need to spend more time socializing. Outgoing Sims have more social options. For example, they're more likely to dance, flirt, give backrubs, hug, entertain, compliment, brag, and tickle. They also respond more positively to these social interactions than shy people do.

Fig. 2-3. Outgoing Sims enjoy backrubs and other highly social give-and-take activities. They're also more likely to join a group activity.

Fig. 2-4. Shy Sims (with low Outgoing points) prefer simpler interactions, such as playing in the fountain.

They have no compunction about joining others in games, dance, or the hot tub. Finally, they get more fun out of watching Romance on TV.

Shy people, on the other hand, prefer more solitary fun. Less outgoing folks would rather play in a fountain, and they're less likely to accept a hug or a backrub from another Sim. Shy Sims do need social interaction from time to time, however.

Top Secret Hot Tub Tip

Here's a little detail *everybody* will be asking about. Only *you* will know the answer, though, because you were savvy enough to buy this strategy guide. Our inside source is none other than Will Wright.

Will says, "If the first Sim to get into your hot tub has a high Outgoing rating (7 or above), he or she climbs in naked; otherwise, he or she wears a swimsuit. Anyone who enters the hot tub after that wears whatever the first person did."

Tips from the Testers

I recommend always maxing out Outgoing and Nice attributes. The social aspect is extremely difficult without these stats—and practically impossible in cases where there are no Outgoing and Nice points allocated to a Sim's personality. With Nice and Outgoing maxed out, your Sim can often build a relationship to 100 the first time he or she meets a visiting Sim.

—Andrew Blomquist, Tester

Active/Lazy

Sims with high Active ratings are drawn to activities such as shooting hoops, swimming in the backyard pool, and dancing at the stereo. Active Sim kids love to play on the outdoor play structure. And Active Sims naturally have the most fun watching Action shows on TV.

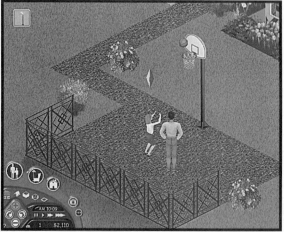

Fig. 2-5. Active Sims love to dance, dive into swimming pools, and shoot hoops.

Fig. 2-6. Lazy Sims are real couch potatoes. TV-watching and just sitting are among their favorite activities.

The Comfort motive score drops faster for lazy Sims. Thus, they should spend more quality time just sitting around. Lazy folks are more likely to nap in recliners or on sofas, watch TV, or soak in a hot tub. Wakeup time is longer for the lazy Sim, too, whereas active Sims practically leap out of bed.

Playful/Serious

Playful Sims have more social options than serious Sims do. They're more likely to entertain, joke, tickle, or scare other Sims, and they also respond more positively to such interactions. Playful Sims like to play with a baby, dollhouse, or computer game, shoot a game of pool, or fire up the pinball machine. They may even get a kick out of gazing at the goofy lawn flamingo. Playful Sim kids love to join in games of tag, scramble around on the backyard play structure, and play with toy boxes and train sets.

NOTE
Although Sim kids inherit their individual personalities from their parents, in general they value fun more than adults.

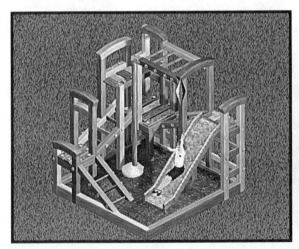

Fig. 2-7. Playful Sims love games, jokes, tickling, and other high-spirited interactions. Kids, in particular, love fun activities.

Fig. 2-8. Serious Sims prefer to cozy up with a book or a quiet game of chess. They also have a higher appreciation of art objects.

At the other end of the scale, more serious types would rather read a book or newspaper, play chess, or view a painting or sculpture.

Nice/Grouchy

Sims at the high end of the Nice scale are more likely to cheer up a moody friend or give a backrub, gift, or compliment. Nice Sims also like to tuck in their kids. Now, isn't that nice?

Sims at the Grouchy end of the scale are more inclined to brag, insult, slap, scare, or even attack other Sims. Grouchy Sims may even take a perverse pleasure in kicking a lawn flamingo or stomping on garden flowers.

Fig. 2-9. What could satisfy a grouchy Sim more than kicking a stupid lawn flamingo?

How Personality Affects Fun

Fig. 2-10. The more playful your Sims, the more Fun points they can earn engaging in Fun activities.

Interacting with certain objects can increase a Sim's Fun score. Although each object's point increase has a limit, certain personality traits raise the maximum Fun points a Sim can earn by as many as 10. To learn more about motive max, see "Mood and Motives."

TRAITS THAT RAISE MAX FUN VALUE

PERSONALITY TRAIT	RAISES MAX FUN SCORE FOR
Playful	Aquarium, Chess Table, Computer, Doll House, Flamingo, Pinball, TV (Cartoon Channel), VR Glasses
Serious (Low Playful)	Newspaper (Read)
Active	Basketball Hoop, Play Structure, TV (Action Channel)
Outgoing	Hot Tub, TV (Romance Channel)
Grouchy (Low Nice)	TV (Horror Channel)

How Personality Affects Skill Building

Sims can't advance in their world without increasing certain skills. They do so by using "skill-building" objects. Good news! Some personality traits accelerate the speed with which they acquire some skills.

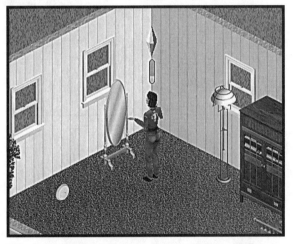

Fig. 2-11. Outgoing Sims can build Charisma skill (by practicing speeches at mirrors) faster than shy Sims can.

SKILLS ACCELERATED BY PERSONALITY

SKILL	OBJECTS USED TO INCREASE SKILL	TRAIT ACCELERATOR
Creativity	Easel, Piano	Playful
Body	Exercise Machine, Swimming Pool	Active
Charisma	Medicine Cabinet, Mirrors	Outgoing

Sim Zodiac Signs

When you assign points to the five Personality traits, you also create a zodiac sign for your Sim. Each zodiac sign also has a preconfigured trait "prototype." Will Wright and his team created these, and then tested every possible combination extensively to determine which signs got along best. The following table shows the results.

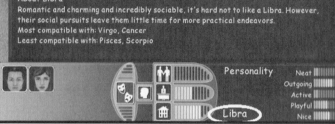

Fig. 2-12. Click on Personality, and then on a zodiac sign, to learn which signs your Sim is most or least compatible with.

SIM ZODIAC SIGNS

SIGN	ATTRACTED TO	REPELLED BY
Virgo	Aquarius/Sagittarius	Leo/Taurus
Libra	Virgo/Cancer	Pisces/Scorpio
Scorpio	Pisces/Leo	Libra/Aquarius
Sagittarius	Pisces/Capricorn	Libra/Scorpio
Leo	Sagittarius/Cancer	Capricorn/Gemini
Capricorn	Aquarius/Taurus	Leo/Gemini
Aquarius	Capricorn/Sagittarius	Scorpio/Virgo
Pisces	Scorpio/Gemini	Leo/Aries
Aries	Gemini/Taurus	Cancer/Libra
Taurus	Aries/Libra	Virgo/Cancer
Gemini	Pisces/Virgo	Capricorn/Aries
Cancer	Taurus/Scorpio	Gemini/Aries

> **NOTE**
> When creating a character, you can click on the zodiac to cycle through the different signs. It will automatically set the personality traits to reflect that sign.

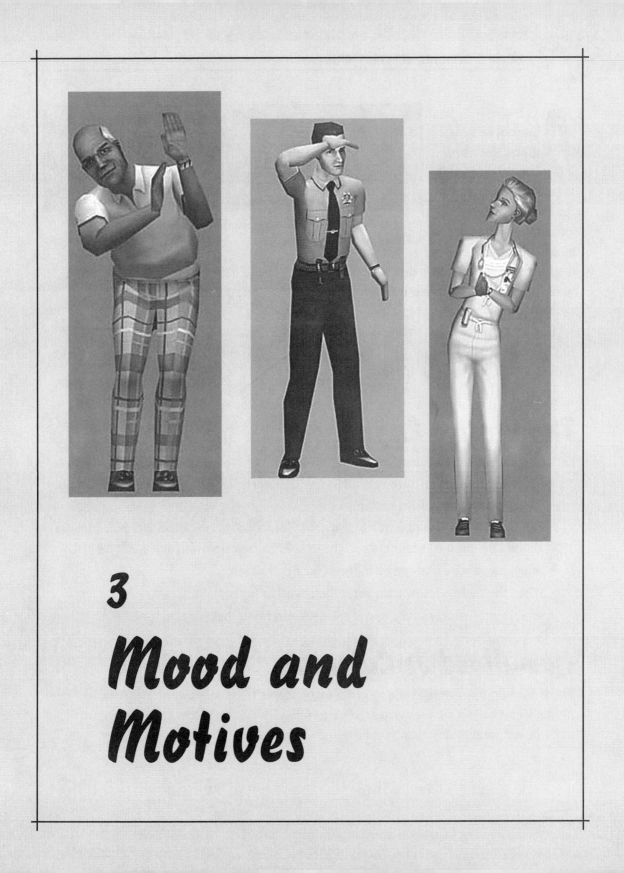

3

Mood and Motives

Fig. 3-1. To keep your Sims happy, monitor their needs closely in the Control Panel's Mood display.

As *The Sims* manual tells you, green Mood bars indicate a good mood (a state of happiness), and red Mood bars indicate a bad mood. Then, with tongue firmly in cheek, it suggests that each Sim's disposition reflects "a concatenation of various mood conditions and attributes, filtered through a fiendishly complicated computing formula reflecting the grandiose sophistication of the game."

But, of course, any self-respecting strategy guide must peek under the hood at the Engine. So we made our way to Maxis in Walnut Creek, California, to meet with Will Wright and dig up some inside info.

Guess what? His computing formulas are fiendishly complicated.

The Motive Engine

Let's start with a quick review:

- Eight basic needs, or "motives"—Hunger, Comfort, Hygiene, Bladder, Energy, Fun, Social, and Room—drive each Sim.
- Each motive displays as a horizontal color bar depicting a scale of 200 points, from 100 (totally fulfilled need) at far right to -100 (totally unfulfilled need) at far left.
- When the motive is above zero, the color bar is green.
- When the motive is less than zero, the color bar is red.
- When a motive drops very low, it's time to attend to that particular need.

How Mood Is Calculated

The Motive Engine averages the motives' eight scores to calculate your Sim's Mood rating. But it's not a simple average. It's a *weighted* average: that is, each motive carries more or less weight, depending on how high or low it is. For example, a very low Hunger score puts a Sim on the verge of death. So naturally, the lower the Hunger score drops, the more weight it carries in the Mood calculation.

Makes sense, doesn't it? Even with all your other needs (Fun, Social, etc.) maxed out in the green, your own mood would be pretty low if you were starving. The same is true of the Bladder motive: the greater *anybody's* bladder need, the greater its weight in the mood calculation.

Fig. 3-2. The Mood bars reflect a "weighted average" of all other Needs states. Each bar represents a 20-point increment on the Mood scale from -100 to 100.

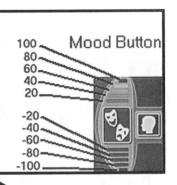

TIP

Physical needs gain considerable weight the lower they drop. Very low Hunger, Bladder, or Comfort scores will lower a mood considerably. Sometimes a simple meal, a trip to the toilet, or a rest in a comfy chair can raise a mood several bars higher.

The "Happy Weights" Charts

Caution: Stop here if numbers hurt you! Believe me, casual players certainly know all they need to know about how a Sim's mood is determined. Again, the basic concept is this: the lower or higher a motive score is, the more weight it carries in the game's mood calculation. Scores associated with physical needs—Hunger primarily, but also Comfort and Bladder—are weighted heavier than others as they plunge lower into the red. On the other hand, a Social score of 100 can have a dramatic effect on mood as well.

But all you number-crunchers and engine-tinkerers, follow us in. A Sim's Mood score, as mentioned, is calculated as a weighted average of that Sim's eight motive scores. Specifically, this means each of the eight motive scores is multiplied by a value (thus, "weighted") that corresponds to how high or low that motive score is at the moment. After these multipliers have modified all eight motive scores, they're averaged to calculate the Mood score. (To see how the Mood point score translates into the 10 Mood bars, refer to Figure 3-2.)

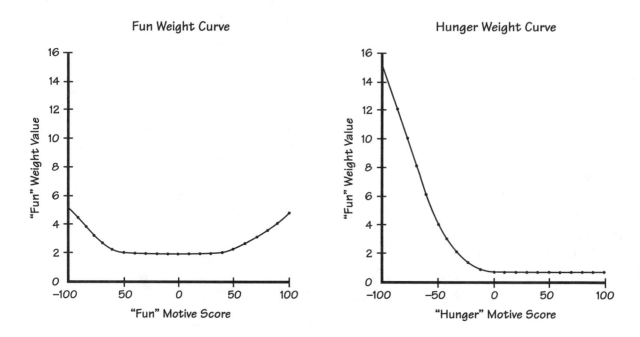

Fun Weight Curve

Hunger Weight Curve

The following graphs depict the multipliers (weights) used in the mood calculation for two very different motives, Hunger and Fun. Again, physical needs such as Hunger, Comfort, and Bladder carry the most weight when their scores get low. On the other hand, Fun and Social considerations gain weight as the overall Mood score rises.

Again, it makes sense, doesn't it?

As you can see, the lower a Sim's Hunger score, the higher the multiplier. Indeed, the upward curve is quite steep as the Sim approaches the starvation score of -100. As Hunger drops from -60 to -100, the multiplier shoots up from 5 to 15! So when a Sim's Hunger score hits, say, -99 (moments before grisly death), the mood calculation multiplies -99 times 14.75 when averaging the motive scores.

That's lot of negative points to average in. Thus, you can see how weighted it is, and how being really hungry drags mood right down into the red.

On the other hand, as Hunger and Fun motive scores increase, the weight, or multiplier, for Fun grows more important. In fact, at higher motive scores, Fun carries from three to five times more weight than Hunger. (The Hunger weight stays at 1 after the Hunger motive score crosses zero into the green region.) Again, when your belly is full, you forget about food and think about fun.

A Sim's Eight Basic Needs

Yes, Sims have eight needs. They satisfy these needs by interacting with objects or other Sims. As a rule, consult the ratings in the game's Buy mode catalog to see how well a given object will satisfy a given need. The higher the rating, the better the object will satisfy the motive (need) listed.

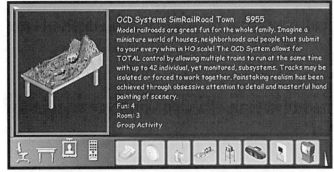

Fig. 3-3. Check the Buy mode catalog to learn which objects boost which motives. This model railroad is fun, enhances the room, and attracts a crowd.

The Max [Motive] Factor

But not only do different objects increase motives at different speeds, many objects can bring only the motive they satisfy to a certain maximum value. When your Sims hit this "Max [Motive]" value, they disengage from the activity (except in a few special skill-building activities). This Max [Motive] factor is why Sims sometimes don't take whole-heartedly to the activities you select for them.

Motive Decay

Motives, of course, decay over time, creating increasingly dire needs. We'll discuss the various motives in more depth later in the chapter. For now, read on for some quick tips on how motive decay works.

- Most motives decay more slowly while Sims sleep or work.
- Comfort decays more quickly for Lazy (low Active) people.
- Social decays more quickly for Outgoing people.
- Energy decays at a constant rate, except when strenuous physical activity accelerates it.
- Bladder decays at a constant rate, except when food or beverage consumption stimulates it.
- Hunger decay slows *considerably* as the Hunger score approaches the bottom of the scale.
- Fun decays more quickly for kids.

Hunger: The Food Chain Revealed

Hunger is the primal need, the one at the bottom of Maslow's pyramid, the foundation of all other needs, the one you can least afford to ignore. Much of life is organized around the regular consumption of food. *The Sims* is no different. So here's a step-by-step look at what the Maxis design team calls the "food chain."

First, Get a Refrigerator!

In *The Sims,* the food chain starts at the refrigerator. Basically, without a fridge, your Sims have very few food options—Pizza and Grilling. Subsisting on pizza might not sound so bad at first. But really—pizza for *every* meal? Scary. And pizza is expensive, too. At §40 a pie, it adds up, costing far more than a fridge over time. And you have to wait an hour for delivery. And deal with Freddy the Pizza Dude.

Hey, *get a refrigerator*. First thing. Trust us on this one.

Fig. 3-4. The food chain in THE SIMS starts at the refrigerator. Without a fridge, your only food options are pizza delivery and grilling.

Food Prep

Once your Sim gets a fridge and grabs ingredients for a meal, the next link in the food chain is the food prep area. Sims can prepare food in only two places—on a counter or in a food processor. Sims won't use tables or desks for food prep. Nor will they prepare food on counters cluttered with other stuff—dirty plates, pizza boxes, newspapers, piles of bills, or other appliances, such as coffeemakers. If no food prep area is available, your Sim stands in the kitchen with great pathos, eating cold beans from a can.

TIP

If your Sim raids the fridge and ends up eating a can of beans, you have no food prep area available. Sims prepare far more nourishing meals on an open counter or in a food processor.

Counters

First, all counters are created equal. Upgrading to expensive counters does not enhance the food prep process in any way, so counter-buying is an aesthetic choice and nothing else. Using *any* counter for food prep adds 16 points to the meal's Hunger motive.

All counters have equal effect on the time it takes to prepare the food, too. Only Cooking skill affect meal prep time.

Food Processors

Food processors prepare more satisfying meals than do counters because they add 32 points to the meal's Hunger motive— twice the increase of countertop food prep. They also prepare food faster than you would be able to on a counter. As with counters, prep time is modified by Cooking skill.

XLR8R Food Processor $220
Part of the Intelli-kitchen total food prep system, the XLR8R accelerates food delivery time...AND taste. The low-cost, high-precision pulse-echo radar blades enable invariable food chunk tolerances by combining digital logic with microwave techniques. Sealed housing. Quick lock lid. Finger Shield. Idi-Pruuf control panel.
Hunger: 2

Fig. 3-5. Counters are fine for prep work, but the trusty XLR8R food processor adds more to your meal.

Cooking Appliances

OK, you've prepped the food. Now what? Naturally, your Sim looks for someplace to cook it. Sims can cook food in the toaster oven, microwave, or on one of two stoves. Both the microwave and the toaster oven take the same

NOTE
In a pinch, your Sim can prepare meals atop dishwashers or trash compactors. Each of these items adds only 5 points to the meal's Hunger score increase, however.

amount of time to cook your meal. If your Sim finds no cooking appliance—well, enjoy your salad, pal—or the "quick meal" equivalent, a Box o' Cold Yuck. Note that when you cook a meal, your Sim's Cooking skill affects both cooking time and Hunger point increase.

Stoves

The two stove models are the Dialectric free-standing range (adds 32 points to the meal's Hunger motive) and the more expensive Pyrotorre gas range (adds 40 points). Additionally, each stove adds the following to the Hunger motive: 1.5 x Cooking skill.

Careful, though. Low-skill cooks stand a good chance of starting a cooking fire. (See "Fire, Theft, and Accidents" in the "Sim Economics" section.)

Toaster Oven

The wonderfully cheap Brand Name toaster oven is worth a mere 9 Hunger points to your meal. Add to that your Sim's current Cooking skill to determine your meal's total Hunger motive increase. Poor cooks can start a fire with ease in this baby. Every meal cooked in the toaster oven takes the same amount of time—five game minutes.

Microwave

The Positive Potential microwave uses its "neo-nonionizing radiation in a magnetron tube to enable half-wave voltage octupling." And that means good food! This glowing technology zaps 16 points into the meal; add your Sim's Cooking skill to determine its total Hunger motive increase. Sims won't start fires with the microwave, although they may irradiate much of the tri-state area.

Fig. 3-6. The top-of-the-line Pyrotorre gas range adds a hefty 48 Hunger points to any cooked meal.

Barbecue Grill

The Wild Bill THX-451 barbecue is a special part of the food chain. Burgers start and end here. Its single available interaction, "Grill," includes the prep and cooking of a group platter of six meals. Grilling adds 16 points to the Hunger motive increase for each barbecued meal.

Any cook can start a BBQ fire; cooking skill is irrelevant. It is the proximity of other objects that is the biggest fire risk.

How Appliances and Food Prep Surfaces Affect Hunger Score

As the foregoing descriptions demonstrate, each prep surface or appliance adds points to the meal's Hunger motive. We gathered all those values into a single table because, well, that's the type of guys we are:

HOW APPLIANCES AND SURFACES AFFECT HUNGER SCORE

APPLIANCE/SURFACE	HUNGER POINTS ADDED TO MEAL
Fridge (Llamark)	9
Fridge (Porcina)	12
Fridge (Freeze Secret)	16
Counter (NuMica)	16
Counter (Tiled)	16
Counter (Barcelona)	16
Food Processor	32
Dishwasher	5
Trash Compactor	5
Stove (Dialectric)	32 (plus 1.5 x Cooking skill)
Stove (Pyrotorre)	48 (plus 1.5 x Cooking skill)
Microwave	16 (plus Cooking skill)
Toaster Oven	9 (plus Cooking skill)

Food!

OK, time to gorge—on food data, that is. Here's where you learn everything about food items in *The Sims*—cost, types, Hunger points, spoilage rates, and other succulent tidbits of information.

Cost of Meals

Five meal types cost money in *The Sims*.

- Snack: $5
- Meal: $10
- Group Meal: $20
- Barbecue Meal: $20
- Pizza: $40

Hunger Score for Each Meal

In addition to all the Hunger motive points various prep and cooking methods add, each meal type has its own Hunger point value.

MEAL TYPE	HUNGER MOTIVE POINTS
Snack	9
Quick Meal	16
Full Meal	16
Group Meal (Per Serving)	16
Pizza (Per Serving)	33

Food Types

The Sims offers a surprising variety of foods for your munching pleasure. The same meal type can manifest several ways, depending on food prep (or lack thereof) and cooking appliance (or lack thereof). And not all food in *The Sims* is a "meal." Fridge snacks and food gifts from visitors (candy or fruitcakes) add Hunger points, too. Here's a quick rundown of all the game's food types.

Pizza

Ah, pizza. Favored food of game designers and Q & A testers everywhere. In The Sims, the only source of pizza is Freddy the Pizza Dude. To order, simply pick up the phone and, under Services, select Pizza. Freddy arrives with your $40 pie within the hour.

Six slices of pizza come in each box. Pizza offers a stout 33 Hunger points per slice. (This may seem like a lot, but remember that pizza servings aren't enhanced, point-wise, by prep and cooking.) Once delivered, the pizza box can be placed on the ground. But Sims only eat while standing. Neat Sims wash their hands after a greasy pizza-fest.

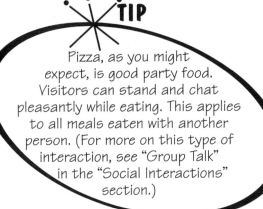

TIP

Pizza, as you might expect, is good party food. Visitors can stand and chat pleasantly while eating. This applies to all meals eaten with another person. (For more on this type of interaction, see "Group Talk" in the "Social Interactions" section.)

Fig. 3-7. Pizza hits the spot when you don't have time to cook. Here, the gals chow down and chat about soccer.

Have Snack

Snacks come directly from the refrigerator, require no prep or cooking, and give a quick (if small) burst of Hunger satisfaction. Sims grab a snack from the fridge and eat it right away, while standing. Each snack offers 9 Hunger points by itself; include the points offered by the refrigerator model to determine total Hunger motive increase.

Have Quick Breakfast/Lunch/Dinner

This light meal is taken from the fridge as a closed box and requires no prep. Your Sim either cooks it or, if no cooking appliance is available, stands and eats right from the box. If cooked, the Quick Meal may be eaten

Fig. 3-8. Snacks are good for a quick Hunger fix. Kids can't cook, but they can help themselves to snacks.

sitting or standing. The Hunger motive increase is 16 points plus the points added by the refrigerator model and (if any) the cooking device.

Have Breakfast/Lunch/Dinner

This is a full, single meal. Depending on prep and cooking, it can be beans, salad, or a steak dinner. Sims take the unprepared ingredients from the fridge and search for a prep surface or food processor.

Fig. 3-9. You need a countertop surface or a food processor to chop up the ingredients for a Full Meal.

- If no prep surface is available, the meal morphs into a sorry can of cold beans, which the Sim eats immediately while standing. This is worth 16 Hunger points plus the points added by the refrigerator model—no better than a Quick Meal, actually.

- If a prep surface is available, the Sim uses it to chop up the ingredients. Then the Sim picks up the prepared food and searches for a cooking appliance. If none is found, the meal becomes a plate of salad. This is worth 16 Hunger points, plus the points added by the refrigerator model and the prep surface. Salad can be eaten sitting or standing.

- If the Sim finds a cooking appliance, the prepared food morphs into a "cooking state" (pot for stoves, tray for toaster oven or microwave). The Sim cooks the food; once it's removed from the appliance, it becomes a single plate of food—a steak dinner. This meal is worth 16 Hunger points plus the points added by refrigerator model, prep surface, and cooking appliance (which includes Cooking skill points). A steak dinner may be eaten sitting or standing.

Serve Breakfast/Lunch/Dinner (Group Meal)

This is a full platter of food with six servings. Depending on prep and cooking, it can be beans, salad, or a steak dinner. To start a Group Meal, Sims take unprepared ingredients from the fridge and search for a prep surface or food processor.

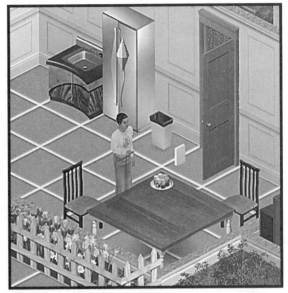

- If no prep surface is available, the meal morphs into a platter of—wow—cans of beans. Your friends will go wild. Each serving of this rare feast increases the eater's Hunger motive score by 16 points plus the points added by the refrigerator model.

- Then the Sim picks up the prepared food and searches for a cooking appliance. If none is found, the meal becomes a group platter of salad. Each serving is worth 16 Hunger points, plus the points added by the refrigerator model and the prep surface.

- If the Sim finds a cooking appliance, the prepared food morphs into a "cooking state" (pot for stoves, tray

Fig. 3-10. Nothing's more pathetic than a guy serving guests a platter full of cans of beans. Get a counter and a cooking appliance, fool!

for toaster oven or microwave). The Sim cooks the food; when it's removed from the appliance, it becomes a group platter of food—steak dinners! Each serving is worth 16 Hunger points plus the points added by refrigerator model, prep surface, and cooking appliance (which includes Cooking skill points).

Gift Food Items

Visitors bearing gifts may offer two kinds of multiple-serving treats—candy and fruitcake.

Candy Box: Offers 12 servings per box. Can be placed on floor but eaten only if set on a table-height serving surface. Each serving offers 3 Hunger points. Always eaten standing up.

Fruitcake: Offers six festive slices. If not eaten, may be used as doorstop. OK, maybe not, but it *can* be served from both table-height surfaces *and* floor. Each serving adds 7 Hunger points. Never goes bad with flies. Really. Always eaten standing up. (Only way to swallow it, apparently.) Neat Sims wash hands afterward, as would any intelligent being. Sims with a high cooking skill enjoy fruitcake more.

After-Meal Cleanup (Or Not)

Sloppy Sims leave dirty plates, pizza boxes, snack bags and other trash lying around the kitchen. (They drop snack bags on the floor, where each creates a small pile of trash.)

Neat Sims, on the other hand, wash the dishes (or load the dishwasher) and throw away trash. When throwing away trash, a Sim picks up the pile (it becomes a plastic trash bag) and seeks to dispose of it in the following order:

1. Indoor trash can or trash compactor. If full, then:
2. Existing trash pile. If full, then:
3. Outdoor trash can.

Dirty dishes and platters, Quick Meal boxes, and pizza boxes spawn flies after eight hours. All uneaten food goes bad and spawns flies after eight hours, too. Candy goes bad after 24 hours. Again, fruitcake never goes bad. We think it has a half-life of 1,300 years, but Maxis won't confirm this.

Fig. 3-11. Bob's kitchen is a mess! Dirty dishes and other garbage attracts flies after eight hours.

Comfort

Comfort is a straightforward need. To be comfortable, Sims need good furniture for seating or sleeping. In general, the better the chair or sofa or bed, the more Comfort satisfaction it provides. But note that a nice hot bath can provide excellent Comfort, too. In fact, a luxurious soak in the $3,200 Hydrothera bathtub boosts your Comfort as high as almost any other item in the catalog.

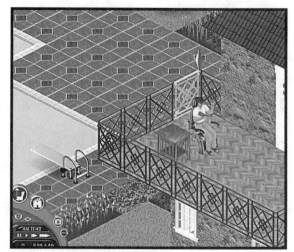

Fig. 3-12. Really, what could be more comforting than reading a book on a balcony overlooking a pool while sitting in the maxi-comfort Von Braun recliner? Answer: Nothing.

Sims may acquire Comfort in tandem with other needs. Tubs boost Comfort and Hygiene at the same time. Beds boost Comfort and Energy at the same time. And, in some cases, you can build skills while boosting Comfort levels. (See the corresponding Tip.)

TIP

Buy nice, comfy chairs for your chess set and dining room, and a good couch for your TV. This way you raise your Comfort score while you build skills or take care of other "sit-down" needs.

Hygiene and Bladder

As a strategy guide, we feel badly when we can find little to say about certain aspects of a game. But really, what could be less tricky than Hygiene and Bladder needs? These two motives are so uncomplicated that we combined them into one section.

To raise Hygiene scores, engage your Sims in activities that clean them. Sneaky, eh? Take showers or baths to max out Hygiene. For quick boosts, go to the sink and wash hands, or use the medicine cabinet to brush teeth. You also gain a decent Hygiene boost from soaking in the hot tub.

TIP

Sims in the Pro Athlete career track suffer the greatest degradation of Hygiene during the course of the workday.

Fig. 3-13. Oops. This guy should have gotten up sooner. Maybe he would have made it to the bathroom.

To relieve the Bladder motive, you have two simple choices: use the toilet or have an accident. Bladder accidents provide full relief, but they leave an unsightly puddle and (as you might expect) push the soiled Sim's Hygiene score to the red end of the scale.

Fun

Fun is a personal, individual thing. Your idea of fun might be different from mine. And gee, isn't that what makes the world go 'round? This diversity is recognized in *The Sims*. As we discussed at length in the foregoing "Personality" section, each Sim's personality structure (particularly the Playful trait) determines the activities a Sim will find most fun.

A simple example: Playful Sims are attracted to computer games, pinball, and dollhouses. Serious Sims—that is, Sims with a low Playful rating—tend to seek activities such as chess, reading, and viewing art objects. To fully understand how activities "broadcast" fun to Sims, check out "Advertising" in the "Autonomy" section.

Max Fun

Activities that provide fun usually have a maximum fun (Max Fun) value—that is, a limit to how high that activity can raise the Fun motive score. Again, personality can affect Max Fun by raising or lowering it for a particular activity.

TV and Fun

TV channels offer differing amounts of fun, depending on Sim personality. Here's a quick look at the TV fare certain Sim types prefer.

TIP

Most fun objects have a maximum fun level. If a Sim's Fun is at 75, and the stereo's Max Fun is at 80, the Sim will only *dance* until he hits 80 Fun points. At that point, he would have to interact with an object that has a Max Fun score higher than 80 in order to get any more Fun.

TYPE OF SIM	PREFERRED TV CHANNEL
Playful	Cartoon
Grouchy (Low Nice)	Horror
Active	Action
Outgoing	Romance

Although TV channels affect the amount of fun Sims get from TV watching, the same isn't true of their choice of genre in music. A Sim has no preference for music types—country over classical, for example, or rock over latin.

Kids and Fun

Fun matters more to kids, in general. Compared to adults, fun plays a bigger part in determining their mood and it drains quickly, so kids have to do fun stuff a lot.

Energy

Energy is the third of physical motive (along with Hunger and Bladder) you can't ignore if it drops very low. If an Energy score bottoms out at -100, the Sim will keel over backward and fall dead asleep on the floor…or sleep standing up, if there's no floor space. It's kind of amusing the first time it happens. After that, it's just sad.

> **NOTE**
>
> Sims actually have a hidden "relationship score" with the beds you place in their house. Every time a Sim sleeps in a bed, his or her attraction to that bed increases, making it more likely they will seek out that bed autonomously the next time they sleep. Thus, you can actually "train" your Sims to sleep in a specific bed.

The main way to replenish your Energy need is to sleep or nap, although coffee or espresso will give you a small shot of Energy. Sleep on any bed, or nap on any sofa or recliner chair.

Tips from the Testers

A profoundly limiting factor is the time constraint sleep puts on your busy Sims—too much to do, not enough Energy to do it. The less time your Sims spend sleeping, the better. One solution: get the most

Modern Mission Bed $3,000
Patterned on the Arts and Crafts movement's design principles of simplicity and workmanship, our craftspeople have reinterpreted this aesthetic for the new millennium. Cherrywood and mahogany combine to create a luxurious place to sleep and re-energize.
Comfort: 9
Energy: 10
Room: 3

Fig. 3-14. The Modern Mission Bed is a modern miracle of design, offering the best Energy boost known to Simdom—a perfect 10!

expensive bed as soon as possible. The Modern Mission bed boosts your Energy score faster during sleep. Thus, you can rise earlier and get more things done before going to work.

—Andrew Blomquist, Tester

Sleep

Sims spin happily into PJs before they go to sleep in bed. Generally, a Sim sleeps until "fully rested"—that is, until their Energy score hits a full 100. At night, however, Sims sleep until at least 6 a.m. regardless of whether or not they're fully rested. There is one way around this: if you queue something up behind sleep, when the Energy score reaches a full 100 points in the middle of the night, a Sim will get up, even if it's before 6 a.m.

Waking Up

In general, waking from sleep is long and slow for Lazy Sims, quicker for Active Sims. Sims arise in a cranky mood if you awaken them before they're full rested (before their Energy score hits a full 100). Sims don't like being awakened by something noisy, either. Alarms going off in the room—clock, fire, or burglar—wake up both adults and kids. So does a fire.

Other events also wake adults, but not kids, if they occur in the same room: baby crying; TV or stereo/radio on; phone ringing; Sim death; Sim playing piano, pinball, or computer game; Sim on exercise machine. Oh, and one other sound awakens adult Sims—a ghostly howl. (See "Ghosts!" in the "Social Interactions" section.)

Using the Alarm Clock

If you have an alarm clock in the room, you may select Set Alarm. When you set an alarm clock, it rings two hours before the car-pool arrival time of any sleeping Sim in the room. However, note that the alarm awakens *everyone* in the room, regardless of car-pool time or whether they're asleep on floor, couch, or bed. (It doesn't matter who set the alarm.) Also, the alarm will go off once for each employed Sim sleeping in the room, even if they have different car-pool times.

Once set, an alarm clock remains set until you direct a Sim to Unset Alarm.

Social

The Social motive is a powerful one in *The Sims*. And why not? As Will Wright comments in the foreword: "There seems to be some evidence that our intelligence is the result of a vicious feedback cycle, a cycle that begins with social behavior....Most of the other high intelligence animals on Earth also seem to be highly social creatures (i.e. dolphins, chimpanzees)."

TIP

Sims don't need neighbors to keep their Social motive high. Just one family member can provide all of the needed interactions. But without friends from outside the family, Sims can't climb very high in any career track.

Because the social aspect of *The Sims* is integral to the game experience, we devoted an entire chapter to social interactions. For now, we simply point out that most interactions with other Sims affect your Sim's Social motive score. For an in-depth look at interactions that affect the Social motive, see the "Social Interactions" section.

Room

The Room motive is probably the least pressing. In the weighted average that determines Mood, Room carries far less overall weight (especially at the low end) than do other motives. But a critically low Room score still can pull a Mood level down a bar or two. A Mood hovering around zero can make a lot of difference in job promotion, skill-building, friend-making, and other social activities.

Fig. 3-15. Paintings hung on interior walls can increase a Room score.

Anyway, you love your Sims, right? You created them. You want them to be as happy as possible. So let's look at how Room score works. In general, the following factors influence your Sim's like or dislike for a room:

Room Size: The bigger, the better.

Light Levels: Windows, doors, ambient light (day or night), and lamps impact light levels. The brighter, the better.

Number of Corners: The more, the better. (See the "Building" section.)

Positive and Negative Objects: Refer to the following topic for more on this.

Maintenance is important! Some household items need your care. A wilting violet or murky water in the fish tank are not uncommon. If you want a good Room score, don't forget to do routine maintenance: clean the tank, water the plants.

Tips from the Testers

If you need a quick Room score boost, light a fire in the fireplace. Any lit fireplace can make a huge difference in room score. They work especially well when placed outside and lit just before Sims go to work. Because the outside area counts as one big room, the lighted fireplace may significantly raise your Room score for Sims on their way to work.

—Andrew Blomquist, Tester

Fig. 3-16. A cheery, crackling fire in the fireplace greatly enhances Room score.

Positive/Negative Objects

Many objects have a positive effect on Room scores. The Buy mode catalog gives you a good idea of which these are. Below we've reproduced a super-secret Room Score table we smuggled out of Maxis. (Don't tell them you saw it here, OK?) This table lists every object in the game that affects Room score, positively or negatively. It also lists the point increase or decrease each object causes.

Ha! Try finding something like *that* in an unauthorized strategy guide. Before we hit the table, though, here's a quick summary of objects with a negative impact on Inside Room Score:

- Trash
- Floods
- Dirty plates
- Meals with flies
- Full trash cans/compactors
- Dead plants
- Puddle or ash pile
- Dead fish in aquariums
- Dirty objects (shower, toilet, tub)

> ### Tips from the Testers
> Room Score can have a big impact on how relationships go. Lights help this a lot. The §350 "Torchosteronne" floor lamp is one of the most cost-efficient items you can place to raise Room Scores. Also, build very large rooms if you plan to use them for social activities or gaining skills. Rounding off corners with a few diagonal walls will also help boost scores.
>
> —Jason Morales, Tester

Certain broken objects (computer, TV, pinball) directly lower Room score, too, but others (dishwasher, shower, sink) rely on leaky flooding for negative impact.

Ouside Room Score is a different matter as it has its own algorithm. One factor that influences Ouside Room Score is time of day since the amount of light affects the score (more sunlight, higher score). As for objects, those that would negatively impact the Inside Room Score, will also negatively impact an Outside Room Score. All other objects count positively, once per number of tiles they are.

> NOTE
> Art objects add to Room Score based on their price, which randomly appreciates or depreciates daily.

ROOM SCORE

OBJECT	STATE/TYPE	ROOM SCORE
Aquarium	Fish Alive	25
	Dirty	-25
	Dirty and/or Dead	-50
Ash		-10
Bar		20
Bed	Unmade (Any Bed)	-10
	Made Mission	30
	Made (Any, except Mission)	10
Chair	Parisienne	25
	Empress	10
Clock: Grandfather		50
Computer	Broken	-25
Counter	Barcelona	15
Desk	Redmond	15
Dresser	Antique Armoire	20
	Oak Armoire	10
Fire		-100
Fireplace	Library Edition (Off)	20
	Library Edition (On)	75
	Worcestershire (Off)	15
	Worcestershire (On)	60
	Bostonian (Off)	10
	Bostonian (On)	45
	Modesto (Off)	5
	Modesto (On)	30

ROOM SCORE, continued

OBJECT	STATE/TYPE	ROOM SCORE
Flamingo		10
Flood		-25
Flowers (Outdoor)	Healthy	20
	Dead	-20
Flowers/Plants (Indoor)	Dead	-10
	Healthy	10
	Wilted	0
Food	Snack (Spoiled)	-15
	Fruitcake (Empty Plate)	-5
	BBQ Group Meal (Spoiled)	-20
	BBQ Single Meal (Spoiled)	-15
	Empty Plate	-10
	Pizza Slice (Spoiled)	-10
	Pizza Box (Spoiled)	-25
	Candy (Spoiled)	-5
	Group Meal (Spoiled)	-20
	Meal (Spoiled)	-25
	Quick Meal (Spoiled)	-20
Fountain		25
Gift Flowers	Dead	-10
	Alive	20
Lamp	Not Broken	10
Lava Lamp		20
Newspaper	Old Newspapers	-20
Piano		30
Pinball Machine	Broken	-15
Shower	Broken	-15
Sofa	Deiter or Dolce	20

OBJECT	STATE/TYPE	ROOM SCORE
Stereo	Strings	25
Table	Mesa	15
	Parisienne	25
Toilet	Clogged	-10
Train Set: Small		25
Trash Can: Inside	Full	-20
Trash Compactor	Full	-25
Trash Pile		-20
TV	Soma	20
	Broken (Any TV)	-15

Motive Failure States

If you ignore or intentionally obstruct your Sims' physical needs, bad (and embarrassing) things happen. Of the eight motives, only Hunger, Energy, and Bladder can "fail."

At low levels, Hunger decays very slowly, and it motivates autonomous Sims to eat. So Hunger fails rarely unless you intentionally create a failure situation. The Energy and Bladder motives decrease at a fixed rate, however, and can be further stimulated by particularly draining (or filling) activities.

When Energy fails, your Sim falls asleep on the spot. When Bladder fails, well, take a wild guess. When Hunger fails—see the following topic, "Death."

Death

Ah, yes. The Big Sleep. When you goof up and lose a Sim to one of the mistakes listed below, you get this curious message: "Though the body is gone, the spirit will always remain." Now what do you suppose that means? (Hint: For more on this, see "Ghosts!" at the end of the "Social Interactions" section.)

Rest In Peace

Deepest sympathy! Quo has just died. Though the body is gone, the spirit will always remain.

OK

Fig. 3-17. Rest in peace, Quo. You were a good little guy. Will we ever see Quo again? Read the message carefully.

Tips from the Testers

Need to get rid of an extra Sim or two? Build a small swimming pool (3-by-3) with a ladder. Direct the extra Sims into the pool, and then remove the ladder. When the Sims run out of Energy, they drown. As an bonus, you may sell the resulting tombstones for §5 each.

—Syruss Flyte, Tester

NOTE
Think of extra Sims as those disposable Star Trek guys in Federation uniforms who beam down to the planet surface to be killed by the threat Kirk and Spock vanquish in the end. We just hope Syruss never gets his hands on weapons of mass destruction.

Electrocution

Sims without Mechanical skill should keep their distance from a broken TV. Call a Repairman, instead. With 0 Mechanical points, a Sim stands a 100 percent chance of getting electrocuted if the Sim tries to repair a TV. With 1 skill point, the odds of death drop to 25 percent. With 2 points, the chance is only 10 percent. At every skill level (3 to 10) above that, the chance of electrocution is 1 percent.

Lamps can electrocute, too, if Sims change burned-out lightbulbs. (Outdoor garden lamps require no lightbulb changes.) But the odds are small—only 1 in 100 for every Sim, regardless of Mechanical skill level. After any electrocution, an urn stands where the Sim once stood. Repairmen never get electrocuted.

Fire Death

When Sims die by fire, they flail around and then, in the words of the design spec document, "do a one-tile Wicked Witch 'I'm melting' kind of crumple." (Flames around a burning Sim obstruct most of this animation from view.) A burial urn appears immediately at the end of the gruesome spectacle. Once a Sim is set ablaze, however, another Sim can save him or her with a fire extinguisher. But you'd better be quick about it.

NOTE
Visitors can die by fire, as well.

Fig. 3-18. Sims can live for days with low Hunger and give you plenty of warning that starvation lies ahead. For example, this woman needs a burger, BAD.

Starvation

A Sim's Hunger rating decays very, very slowly at low levels. So it takes Sims a *lo-o-o-o-ong* time to starve to death. Days, in fact. What a pleasant thought! But the point is, Sims don't drop dead suddenly of hunger with little warning. They let you know when they're hungry by waving, yelling, and displaying the "I Need Food!" icon over their heads. And they seek food autonomously (if you have Free Will checked in the Options box) unless you keep them busy otherwise with your Big God Orders, you power-hound.

However, Sims *will* starve if they have no means of obtaining food—no fridge and no money for pizza, or they're trapped somehow by, say, sadistic architecture. When this happens, the poor Sim falls to the floor in the fetal position and turns into a burial urn.

4

Sim Autonomy

As Neighborhood God, your job (unless you choose some capricious Chaldean deity as your role model) is to keep your Sims happy—that is, in a good mood. One way to do this is to micromanage their lives, directing them moment by moment to engage in interactions that fulfill their needs—kind of like most moms.

But a better God is One who truly understands His or Her Sims and their motivations. A Good God creates friendly, efficient environments so Sims can find a measure of happiness on their own, too. We take a closer look here at what Will Wright calls the game's "Happyscape"—the complex internal logic that drives Sims to seek, on their own, the most "happy-making" interaction available.

A Note About the Queue

As *The Sims* manual explains, you can queue as many as eight interactions for each Sim in your household. When left to act autonomously, however, Sims queue only one interaction at a time. They have very small brains, you see. Your Sim performs a chosen interaction, waits a few seconds, and then picks another interaction. However, *your* orders always take precedence. Selecting an interaction for your Sims cancels from the queue any action they may have chosen for themselves.

> **NOTE**
> To cancel any interaction, whether chosen by you or your Sim, click on its icon in the queue. A red X will appear over the icon. When the Sim exits the interaction, the icon will disappear. (Be patient. Sometimes your Sim needs a few seconds to terminate cancelled interactions fully.)

How Sims Make "Free Will" Decisions

In lieu of orders from God (you), Sims with Free Will do their own thing. On the surface, their choices seem straightforward, based on needs. "I'm hungry, so I will eat. My energy is low, so I will sleep." And, in general, that's exactly how it works.

But it's not as simple as just picking the lowest motive score and choosing an activity that increases it. A variety of factors can influence a Sim's calculation of needs. Moreover, in *The Sims*, *objects* actually drive the decision-making process by "advertising" their wondrous benefits to your little people. Some advertise falsely. What exactly does that mean? Read on.

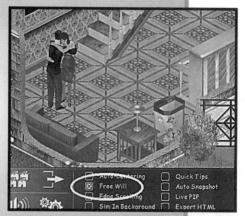

Fig. 4-1. With the Free Will box marked, your Sims live life on THEIR terms unless you step in with your own directives.

Advertising

In essence, each interaction in the household—whether with a couch, a food processor, a lawn flamingo, or another Sim—calls like a carnival barker. "Hey, brush your teeth for Hygiene 25 here!" shouts the bathroom medicine cabinet. "Yo, I got 30 Comfort for a good sit, my man," says the living room's green plaid sofa.

Your autonomous Sim sorts through these tempting offers and selects the four activities that will make him or her happiest. Then, unless one candidate muscles its way to the front of the queue (see the following "Priority Interactions" section), your Sim selects randomly from among them.

Will Wright calls this incessant harangue "advertising." Each potential interaction broadcasts an "ad" touting how happy it can make your Sim by raising a certain motive score.

> **NOTE**
>
> Sim neighbors are "smarter" than the Sims you control in the active household. Visitors always choose the best activity available to raise their mood, unlike your current Sims, who choose randomly from among the top four.

Priority Interactions

Household Sims don't always choose wisely on their own. Because they select randomly from the four highest advertised candidates, one of every four choices will rank lowest.

Priority interactions, however, *always* get picked if they're the highest rated of the four. These include Sleep (highly advertised when the Energy score is low), Use Toilet (highly advertised when Bladder is low), or one of the eat-food commands (Make Dinner, Have Snack, and the like) when Hunger is low.

Fig. 4-2. Using the toilet is a priority interaction for autonomous Sims. That is, Sims select it automatically if it's the highest advertised interaction.

"Push" Interactions

Certain other interactions bypass this sorting process, however. These special choices "push" to the front of the queue, ignoring the top four. These interactions include Wash Hands after eating pizza or using the toilet (for Sims with a high Neat trait); Panic, if a fire breaks out; Go to Work (if the Sim is in a good mood, of course); and Move Out of the Way, if your Sim blocks another Sim's path. Note that you can delete these interactions by deleting them from your Sims queue.

Fig. 4-3. When a fire breaks out, Sims come running in a Panic reaction that pushes its way to the front of the queue regardless of their other needs.

False Advertising

Some interactions advertise falsely. They lure the autonomous Sim by promising fulfillment of a real need, but they don't actually raise that motive score. A good example is

Fig. 4-4. The Mourn interaction advertises powerfully for 24 hours after a Sim death. It lures with false advertising, however, offering a 50-point increase for each of the five needs, but satisfying none!

the phone. When it rings, the interaction "Answer" advertises 50 points each of Fun, Comfort, and Social fulfillment. But the act of answering the phone fulfills none of these needs—not directly, anyway.

Another example is the somber interaction Mourn. In the first 24 hours after a death, a deceased Sim's tombstone or urn advertises a whopping 50 points of Comfort, Fun, Hygiene, Social, and Room! Your household Sims are very motivated to mourn their dearly departed that first day.

Ad Modifiers

Three factors influence an ad's attractiveness—the Sim's personality, current motive scores, and distance from the beckoning object.

How Personality Modifies Choice

The Personality section earlier in this book covered personality influences on Sim behavior in general terms. What follows is a more specific examination of how this works.

When a personality trait "modifies" an activity, it actually raises or lowers the point value of the ad that activity broadcasts. The more points of the trait the Sim has, the more points that trait contributes to the activity's ad.

NOTE

For a complete list of household interactions, their ads, and the personality traits that modify the ads, see the "Object Advertising" table later in this chapter.

Fig. 4-5. Two activities—Turn On (the TV) and Dance (at the boom box)—advertise the same amount of Fun points. Because her Active trait is high, Betty chooses to dance; Bob chooses TV because he's, well, lazy.

Say, for example, a Sim with low Fun points stands in his living room. The big-screen Soma Plasma TV and the Down Wit' Dat boom box sit in the same room. The TV interaction Turn On broadcasts an ad of 49 Fun, and the boom box interaction Dance broadcasts an ad of 50 Fun. Which does your Sim choose?

Other things being equal, the Sim will choose to dance. But other things are rarely equal in *The Sims*. In this case, the choice depends on how many Active points you've assigned to this Sim's personality index. The Active/Lazy scale modifies the amount of Fun points both activities advertise, but in opposite ways. For a Lazy (low Active) Sim, the TV will advertise a high number of points, while an Active Sim's personality will take away points from the TV, so it advertises less. The Active Sim, however, will get more points from the Dance ad. Even if your Sim is just a little on the Lazy side, he'll gravitate to the tube. Of course, an Active Sim looking for Fun points will boogie at the boom box. In the Object Advertising Table later in this section, the values you see are the *highest* they can be. Depending on personality, the ad values may drop for a certain object.

How Motive Scores Modify Ad Choice

Again, household objects advertise an increase in motive scores for certain activities— 35 Fun to play chess, 40 Room to wind the grandfather clock, and so on. Certain personality traits modify these ads a bit. After that, your autonomous Sim chooses activities that offer the greatest score increase, right? Wrong. As the motive score changes, the amount of happiness a Sim derives from raising that score changes, as well.

Whew! This may seem complicated, but it's a basic phenomenon that mirrors your own life decisions and the circumstances that affect them. (We explain in detail how Sims calculate happiness in the following section, "Happiness Contribution Curves.")

If a Sim is very low on both Hunger and Fun, then, which type of ad (Hunger-satis-fying or Fun-satisfying) will most attract his or her attention? Obviously, the best

Fig. 4-6. Your life is dull and you're starving. Which need do you fulfill first? Answer: SNACK TIME! A critical need such as Hunger increases in importance as its score drops.

Hunger ad will carry far more weight. As in real life, the more eating meals raises a Sim's Hunger score, the less appeal Hunger-fulfilling ads will have. After you eat a hearty steak dinner, those mouth-watering food ads on TV have far less allure.

NOTE

Head spinning? Let's throw in yet another variable. It turns out some interactions don't even advertise until a motive reaches a specific level. For example, Sims won't call for pizza delivery autonomously until their Hunger score drops below -75.

Happiness Contribution Curves

OK, if the section on calculating mood with weighted averages in "Mood and Motives" fascinated you, stay with us here. Otherwise, you probably know all you need (or care) to know about how motive scores affect Sim decision-making. Just skip to the "Ad Attenuation" section, because what follows here is for Sim-lovers who want to peel away yet another layer and poke fingers at the innards of Sim autonomy.

First, understand that the happiness an interaction offers your Sim differs from the motive point increase that interaction advertises. Why? Because a curve that calculates a "happiness contribution value" modifies the ad's point increase. Your Sim bases his or her autonomous decisions on this value.

The happiness contribution value is determined using the following steps.

1. Your Sim "hears" the ad for some interaction. The ad offers an increase in some motive score. Let's use two examples for sake of comparison: a refrigerator advertising Hunger 70 to "Have Dinner" and a stereo advertising Fun 70 to "Dance."

2. In essence, your Sim asks, "How happy will a 70-point Hunger increase make me compared to a 70-point Fun increase?" (Of course, she's also comparing the happiness value of numerous other ads, but we'll stick to these two for simplicity's sake.)

3. To determine this, your Sim takes the advertised point increase for each motive (70 Hunger for "Have Dinner" and 70 Fun for "Dance") and converts each into "happiness contribution points." How?

4. First, she determines her current motive scores. For this example, let's say her Fun score is at -20 and her Hunger score has dropped to -70. (Yes, our gal's nearing death.)

5. Now she uses a "happiness contribution curve" (different for each motive) to calculate the happiness contribution of each advertised interaction. These curves (seen below) modify ads depending on the current score of the motive being advertised.

6. Take a look at the following charts. Don't worry, they're straightforward and probably won't hurt you. Note that the graph's horizontal "x-axis" values represent the range of current motive scores (from -100 to 100). The graph's vertical "y-axis" values represent the range of happiness contribution value.

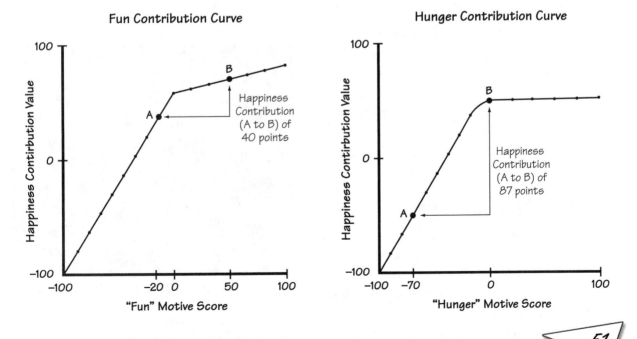

7. Let's calculate the happiness value increase for the "Have Dinner" ad first. On the Hunger graph, find the current motive value on the x-axis—in this case, -70. Then move straight up and mark the point where -70 intersects the Hunger curve. Label it Point A, as we did on our graph above.

8. Now calculate how much your Hunger score will increase if you "Have Dinner." Simple math: Starting at -70 (current Hunger score) on the x-axis, move 70 points to the right along the axis. You end up at 0. This will be your final Hunger score if you eat dinner.

9. Now go straight up and mark where 0 intersects the Hunger curve. Call it Point B.

10. Follow the curve from Point A to Point B. How much is the vertical (y-axis) rise? In this case, you go up from -44 to 43, a total rise of 87 points. This increase is the "happiness contribution value."

11. Follow the same process to plot the happiness contribution value for a "Dance" at the stereo, figuring the "happiness value" rise from the Fun motive's starting score of -20 going up 70 points to 50. In this case, a Fun motive point rise of 70 yields a "happiness value" increase of only 40 points.

12. Thus, even though a stereo dance advertises the same rise in absolute motive points (70), dinner actually increases your very hungry Sim's overall happiness far, far more (87 to 40) in this particular case.

You can see how the happiness contribution curves get steeper in the very low ranges for each motive. This means that when motives get very low, even a small increase in motive points can produce a large happiness contribution value. As in real life, this is particularly true for physical needs such as Hunger, Bladder, and Comfort.

Ad Attenuation

Most ads attenuate over distance. That is, the beckoning interactions grow weaker and eventually dissipate to silence as your Sim moves away from them. Certain ads attenuate less than others, though. For example, a bed's attractiveness remains the same whether a Sim is near or far. On the other

Fig. 4-7. While she stands near her mailbox, this Sim can't "hear" ads for Fun broadcasting from the living room TV or stereo because they attenuate (sort of stretch out and fade) quickly over distance.

hand, most Fun-satisfying objects advertise only to nearby Sims, usually those in the same room.

The Sims measures this attenuation in three increments: ads with high attenuation have a short broadcast range and attract the attention of nearby Sims; ads with medium attenuation broadcast a little farther; Sims can "hear" ads with low attenuation almost anywhere on the lot.

> NOTE
>
> For a complete list of household interactions and their levels of attenuation, see the Object Advertising table later in this chapter.

Most low-attenuation ads are broadcast by activities that fulfill urgent needs—Hunger, Energy, and Bladder. The WhirlWizard hot tub and Aristoscratch pool table are notable exceptions, broadcasting far and wide their ads to Join.

Exit Conditions

A Sim will exit prolonged interactions automatically under certain conditions. Hey, you can only play computer games for so long (unless you're an unmarried programmer). These "exit conditions" allow autonomous Sims to live some

> NOTE
>
> To exit an interaction before it meets exit conditions, click on its icon to delete it from the queue.

semblance of a normal life and not act like little obsessive-compulsive types. Exit conditions also allow you to queue interactions and have your Sim spend some time in each interaction.

When certain motives drop below a critical value, a Sim will exit an interaction. A balloon that pops up over the Sim's head displays an icon to represent the critically low motive. The value differs for household members and visitors.

Fig. 4-8. Sims wave and let you know (using thought balloons) which needs are particularly low. This gal could use a dose of Comfort.

Motive (Sim Type)	Sim Exits Current Interaction When Motive Drops Below
Hunger (Resident)	-80
Hunger (Visitor)	-40
Bladder (Resident)	-85
Bladder (Visitor)	-80
Energy (Resident)	-80
Energy (Visitor)	-70
Comfort (Resident)	-90
Comfort (Visitor)	-60

Additional exit conditions differ slightly for Fun objects, Skill objects, and Repair objects (listed in the following paragraphs.)

Exiting Repair Activities

When a mood score drops below -50 (between two and three red bars on the Mood Indicator), that Sim is too bummed out to continue Repair work on the computer, dishwasher, espresso machine, hot tub, lamp, pinball, shower, sink, toilet, or TV.

Exiting Skill-Building Activities

If a mood score drops below 0 (red bars on the Mood Indicator), that Sim is too depressed to continue honing skills using a bookshelf, chessboard, exercise machine, easel, piano, mirror or medicine cabinet. Also, chess games have a set length: Sims will exit chess when the game ends. (You can just start another game.) And Sims will stop painting at the easel when they finish each work. (To continue, just sell the work and start painting again.)

Fig. 4-9. Bob needs Logic points to advance in his chosen career, but he's too depressed to play chess. Get his motive scores out of the red to cheer him up. Then try again.

> **NOTE**
> Sims exit any Skill-building activity automatically when another interaction is in their queue.

Exiting Fun Activities

In the following Fun activities, Sims will exit the interaction once the Fun score raises the object's maximum points. (Remember, this Max Fun score varies according to a Sim's personality type.)

- Basketball Hoop
- Bookshelf (Read Book)
- Dollhouse
- Computer (Play)
- Pinball Machine
- Play Structure
- Stereo
- Toy Box
- Train Set
- TV
- VR Headset

The following Fun-satisfying interactions offer one-shot interactions that have no exit or refuse conditions. To raise a Fun score to its maximum, a Sim may have to repeat the activity several times.

- Aquarium (Feed or Watch Fish)
- Baby (Play)
- Espresso Machine (Drink)
- Diving Board (Dive In)
- Fountain (View)
- Lava Lamp (View)
- Painting (View)
- Sculpture (View)

The following Fun-satisfying objects have a preset game length. Again, for maximum Fun points, a Sim may have to repeat the activity.

- Chessboard
- Pool Table

Fig. 4-10. Once Sims hop in the hot tub, they tend to hang awhile. In fact, they won't leave autonomously until all four motives satisfied by the experience hit their max.

55

Sims won't exit a hot tub until all the motives it raises (Fun, Comfort, Social, Hygiene) reach their maximum. The pool has no exit conditions; Sims continue swimming until another motive ad calls them out, or you give them another direction.

Object Advertising Table

The following game objects advertise their ability to satisfy Sim needs. The table lists each object alphabetically, and shows the interactions possible with that object, which motive and how many points each interaction advertises, which (if any) personality trait increases the object's ad value, and the level of attenuation for each ad's broadcast.

OBJECT TYPE	POSSIBLE INTERACTIONS	OBJECT VARIATIONS	MOTIVE ADVERTISED	AD VALUE	PERSONALITY TRAIT MODIFIER	AD ATTENUATION
Aquarium						
	Clean & restock					
		Aquarium	Room	30	Neat	Medium
	Feed Fish					
		Aquarium	Room	10	Nice	High
		Aquarium	Fun	10	Playful	High
	Watch Fish					
		Aquarium	Fun	10	Playful	High
Ash						
	Sweep Up					
		Ash	Energy	23		Medium
		Ash	Room	50	Neat	Medium
Baby						
	Play					
		Baby	Fun	50	Playful	Medium

Object Type	Possible Interactions	Object Variations	Motive Advertised	Ad Value	Personality Trait Modifier	Ad Attenuation
Bar						
	Have a drink					
		Bar	Room	30		Low
Barbecue						
	Grill					
		Barbecue	Energy	-10		Low
		Barbecue	Hunger	40	Cooking	Low
Basketball Hoop						
	Join					
		Basketball Hoop	Fun	30	Active	High
		Basketball Hoop	Social	20		Medium
		Basketball Hoop	Energy	-20		Medium
	Play					
		Basketball Hoop	Fun	30	Active	High
		Basketball Hoop	Energy	-20		High
Bed						
	Make Bed					
		All Beds	Room	25	Neat	High
	Sleep					
		Bed double (Cheap Eaze)	Energy	65		None
		Bed double (Napoleon)	Energy	67		None
		Bed double (Mission)	Energy	70		None

57

Object Type	Possible Interactions	Object Variations	Motive Advertised	Ad Value	Personality Trait Modifier	Ad Attenuation
Bed, continued						
	Sleep, continued					
		Bed single (Spartan)	Energy	60		None
		Bed single (Tyke Nyte)	Energy	63		None
	Tuck in kid					
		All Beds	Energy	160	Nice	None
Bookshelf						
	Read a Book					
		Bookshelf (Pine)	Fun	10	Serious	High
		Bookshelf (Amishim)	Fun	20	Serious	High
		Bookshelf (Libri di Regina)	Fun	30	Serious	High
Chair: Living Room						
	Sit					
		Wicker	Comfort	20		Medium
		Country Class	Comfort	20		Medium
		Citronel	Comfort	20		Medium
		Sarrbach	Comfort	20		Medium
Chair: Dining						
	Sit					
		Werkbunnst	Comfort	25		Medium
		Teak	Comfort	25		Medium
		Empress	Comfort	25		Medium
		Parisienne	Comfort	25		Medium

Object Type	Possible Interactions	Object Variations	Motive Advertised	Ad Value	Personality Trait Modifier	Ad Attenuation
Chair: Office/Deck						
	Sit					
		Office Chair	Comfort	20		Medium
		Deck Chair	Comfort	20		Medium
Chair: Recliner						
	Nap					
		Both Recliners	Energy	15	Lazy	High
		Both Recliners	Comfort	20	Lazy	Medium
	Sit					
		Both Recliners	Comfort	30	Lazy	Medium
Chess						
	Join					
		Chess Set	Fun	40	Outgoing	High
		Chess Set	Social	40		Medium
	Play					
		Chess Set	Fun	35	Serious	High
Clock: Grandfather						
	Wind					
		Grandfather Clock	Room	40	Neat	High

Object Type	Possible Interactions	Object Variations	Motive Advertised	Ad Value	Personality Trait Modifier	Ad Attenuation
Coffee Espresso machine						
	Drink Espresso					
		Coffee Espresso machine	Energy	115		Medium
		Coffee Espresso machine	Fun	10		High
		Coffee Espresso machine	Bladder	-10		High
	Repair					
Coffeemaker						
	Drink Coffee					
		Coffeemaker	Bladder	-5		High
		Coffeemaker	Energy	115		Medium
Computer						
	Play					
		Computer (Moneywell)	Fun	30	Playful	High
		Computer (Microscotch)	Fun	35	Playful	High
		Computer (Brahma)	Fun	40	Playful	High
		Computer (Marco)	Fun	50	Playful	High
	Turn Off					
		All Computers	Energy	220	Neat	Medium

OBJECT TYPE	POSSIBLE INTERACTIONS	OBJECT VARIATIONS	MOTIVE ADVERTISED	AD VALUE	PERSONALITY TRAIT MODIFIER	AD ATTENUATION
Dollhouse						
	Play					
		Dollhouse	Fun	30	Playful	High
	Watch					
		Dollhouse	Fun	30	Playful	Medium
		Dollhouse	Social	30		Medium
Easel						
	Paint					
		Easel	Fun	20		High
Flamingo						
	Kick					
		Flamingo	Mood	15	Grouchy	High
	View					
		Flamingo	Fun	10	Playful	High
Flood						
	Clean					
		Flood	Room	80	Neat	High
Flowers (Outdoor)						
	Stomp On					
		All Flowers	Mood	10	Grouchy	High
	Water					
		All Flowers	Room	20	Neat	Medium

Object Type	Possible Interactions	Object Variations	Motive Advertised	Ad Value	Personality Trait Modifier	Ad Attenuation
Flowers/Plants (Indoor)						
	Throw out					
		All Flowers/Plants	Room	50	Neat	Medium
	Water					
		All Flowers/Plants	Room	25	Neat	Medium
Food						
	Clean					
		All Meal/ Snack types	Room	20	Neat	Medium
	Prepare and Eat					
		Food - BBQ Group Meal	Hunger	90		Low
		Food - BBQ Single	Hunger	80		Low
		Food - Candy	Hunger	30		Low
		Food - Fruit Cake Group Meal	Hunger	30		Low
		Food - Fruit Cake Slice	Hunger	80		Low
		Food - Light Meal	Hunger	80		Low
		Food - Pizza Box	Hunger	90		Low
		Food - Pizza Slice	Hunger	80		Low
		Food - Regular Group Meal	Hunger	90		Low
		Food - Regular Meal Single	Hunger	80		Low
		Food - Snack	Hunger	25		Low
Fountain						
	Play					
		Fountain	Fun	10	Shy	High

Object Type	Possible Interactions	Object Variations	Motive Advertised	Ad Value	Personality Trait Modifier	Ad Attenuation
Fridge						
	Have [Meal]					
		All Fridges	Hunger	65		Low
	Have a Snack					
		Llamark	Hunger	20		Low
		Porcina	Hunger	30		Low
		Freeze Secret	Hunger	40		Low
	Have Quick [Meal]					
		All Fridges	Hunger	55		Low
	Serve [Meal]					
		All Fridges	Hunger	70	Cooking	Low
		All Fridges	Energy	-10		Low
Gift Flowers						
	Clean					
		Gift Flowers	Room	30	Neat	Medium
Hot Tub						
	Get in					
		Hot Tub	Fun	45	Lazy	High
		Hot Tub	Comfort	50		High
		Hot Tub	Social	25	Outgoing	Medium
		Hot Tub	Hygiene	5		Medium
	Join					
		Hot Tub	Comfort	30		Low
		Hot Tub	Fun	50	Outgoing	Low
		Hot Tub	Social	50		Low
		Hot Tub	Hygiene	5		Medium

Object Type	Possible Interactions	Object Variations	Motive Advertised	Ad Value	Personality Trait Modifier	Ad Attenuation
Lava Lamp						
	Turn On					
		Lava Lamp	Room	5		High
	View					
		Lava Lamp	Fun	5		High
Mailbox						
	Get Mail					
		Mailbox	Comfort	10		High
		Mailbox	Hunger	10		High
		Mailbox	Hygiene	10		High
		Mailbox	Room	10		High
Medicine Cabinet						
	Brush Teeth					
		Medicine Cabinet	Hygiene	25	Neat	Medium
Newspaper						
	Clean Up					
		Newspaper	Room	50	Neat	Medium
	Read					
		Newspaper	Fun	5	Serious	High
Painting						
	View					
		All Paintings	Fun	5	Serious	High

Object Type	Possible Interactions	Object Variations	Motive Advertised	Ad Value	Personality Trait Modifier	Ad Attenuation
Phone						
	Answer					
		Both Phones	Fun	50		Medium
		Both Phones	Comfort	50		Medium
		Both Phones	Social	50		Medium
	Service/Pizza					
		Both Phones	Hunger	10		Low
Piano						
	Play					
		Piano	Fun	40	S Creativity	High
	Watch					
		Piano	Fun	70		Medium
		Piano	Social	10		Medium
Pinball Machine						
	Join					
		Pinball machine	Fun	50		Medium
		Pinball machine	Social	30		Medium
	Play					
		Pinball machine	Fun	40	Playful	High
Play Structure						
	Join					
		Play Structure	Fun	60	Playful	Medium
		Play Structure	Social	40		Medium
	Play					
		Play Structure	Fun	60	Playful	Medium

Object Type	Possible Interactions	Object Variations	Motive Advertised	Ad Value	Personality Trait Modifier	Ad Attenuation
Pool Diving Board						
	Dive In					
		Pool Diving Board	Fun	35	Active	High
		Pool Diving Board	Energy	-10		High
Pool Table						
	Join					
		Pool Table	Fun	50	Playful	Low
		Pool Table	Social	40		Low
	Play					
		Pool Table	Fun	45	Playful	High
Sculpture						
	View					
		Scylla and Charybdis	Fun	6	Serious	High
		Bust of Athena	Fun	5	Serious	High
		Large Black Slab	Fun	8	Serious	High
		China Vase	Fun	7	Serious	High
Shower						
	Clean					
		Shower	Room	20	Neat	High
	Take a Shower					
		Shower	Hygiene	50	Neat	Medium
Shrub						
Sink						
	Wash Hands					
		All Sinks	Hygiene	10	Neat	High

Object Type	Possible Interactions	Object Variations	Motive Advertised	Ad Value	Personality Trait Modifier	Ad Attenuation
Sofa/Loveseat						
	Nap					
		All Sofas/Loveseats	Energy	40	Lazy	High
		All Sofas/Loveseats	Comfort	5	Lazy	High
	Sit					
		All Sofas/Loveseats	Comfort	30	Lazy	Medium
		Garden Bench	Comfort	30	Lazy	Medium
Stereo						
	Dance					
		Boom Box	Social	40	Outgoing	High
		Boom Box	Fun	50	Active	High
		Zimantz Hi-Fi	Social	50	Outgoing	High
		Zimantz Hi-Fi	Fun	60	Active	High
		Strings Theory	Social	60	Outgoing	High
		Strings Theory	Fun	70	Active	High
	Join					
		Boom Box	Social	40	Outgoing	Low
		Boom Box	Fun	40	Outgoing	Low
		Zimantz Hi-Fi	Social	50	Outgoing	Low
		Zimantz Hi-Fi	Fun	40	Outgoing	Low
		Strings Theory	Social	60	Outgoing	Low
		Strings Theory	Fun	40	Outgoing	Low
	Turn Off					
		All Stereos	Energy	220	Neat	Medium

Object Type	Possible Interactions	Object Variations	Motive Advertised	Ad Value	Personality Trait Modifier	Ad Attenuation
Stereo, continued						
	Turn On					
		Boom Box	Fun	25	Playful	High
		Zimantz Hi-Fi	Fun	25	Playful	High
		Strings Theory	Fun	30	Playful	High
Toilet						
	Clean					
		Both Toilets	Room	40	Neat	High
	Flush					
		Hygeia-O-Matic	Room	30	Neat	High
	Unclog					
		Both Toilets	Room	50	Neat	High
	Use					
		Hygeia-O-Matic	Bladder	50		Low
		Flush Force	Bladder	70		Low
Tombstone/Urn						
	Mourn 1st 24 period					
		Tombstone/Urn	Bladder	5		Low
		Tombstone/Urn	Comfort	50		Low
		Tombstone/Urn	Energy	5		Low
		Tombstone/Urn	Fun	50		Low
		Tombstone/Urn	Hunger	5		Low
		Tombstone/Urn	Hygiene	50		Low
		Tombstone/Urn	Social	50		Low
		Tombstone/Urn	Room	50		Low

Object Type	Possible Interactions	Object Variations	Motive Advertised	Ad Value	Personality Trait Modifier	Ad Attenuation
Tombstone/Urn, continued						
	Mourn 2nd 48 hours					
		Tombstone/Urn	Bladder	0		Low
		Tombstone/Urn	Comfort	30		Low
		Tombstone/Urn	Energy	0		Low
		Tombstone/Urn	Fun	30		Low
		Tombstone/Urn	Hunger	0		Low
		Tombstone/Urn	Hygiene	30		Low
		Tombstone/Urn	Social	30		Low
		Tombstone/Urn	Room	30		Low
Toy Box						
	Play					
		Toy Box	Fun	55	Playful	Medium
Train Set: Large						
	Play					
		Train set large	Fun	40		Medium
	Watch					
		Train set large	Fun	40		Low
		Train set large	Social	40		Low
Train Set: Small						
	Play					
		Train set small	Fun	45	Playful	Medium
	Watch					
		Train set small	Fun	20		Medium
		Train set small	Social	30		Medium

Object Type	Possible Interactions	Object Variations	Motive Advertised	Ad Value	Personality Trait Modifier	Ad Attenuation
Trash Can: Inside						
	Empty trash					
		Trash Can Inside	Room	30	Neat	Medium
Trash Compactor						
	Empty trash					
		Trash Compactor	Room	30		High
Trash Pile						
	Clean					
		Trash Pile	Room	75	Neat	Medium
Tub						
	Clean					
		All Tubs	Room	20	Neat	High
	Take bath					
		Justa	Hygiene	50	Neat	Medium
		Justa	Comfort	20		Medium
		Sani-Queen	Hygiene	60	Neat	Medium
		Sani-Queen	Comfort	25		Medium
		Hydrothera	Hygiene	70	Neat	Medium
		Hydrothera	Comfort	30		Medium
TV						
	Join					
		Monochrome	Fun	20	Lazy	High
		Trottco	Fun	30	Lazy	High
		Soma Plasma	Fun	45	Lazy	High

OBJECT TYPE	POSSIBLE INTERACTIONS	OBJECT VARIATIONS	MOTIVE ADVERTISED	AD VALUE	PERSONALITY TRAIT MODIFIER	AD ATTENUATION
TV, continued						
	Turn Off					
		All TVs	Energy	220	Neat	Medium
	Turn On					
		Monochrome	Fun	18	Lazy	High
		Trottco	Fun	35	Lazy	High
		Soma Plasma	Fun	49	Lazy	High
	Watch TV					
		Monochrome	Fun	18	Lazy	High
		Trottco	Fun	28	Lazy	High
		Soma Plasma	Fun	42	Lazy	High
VR Glasses						
	Play					
		VR Glasses	Fun	60	Playful	High

5

Social
Interactions

Y ou *did* read the game manual, didn't you? Good. Because as we mentioned elsewhere, this guide assumes you know how the basic game interface works; you've
maybe played *The Sims,* maybe a lot. You know how to direct a Sim's actions: click
on an object or on another Sim to bring up a menu of
actions you can perform. The manual calls this a
"pie menu."

This chapter focuses on those menu
choices. We call these *social interactions.*
Why? Because we feel like it. Well, maybe
there's another reason. But we're not going
to tell you because our Mood is low and our
Fun motive is bottoming out. So our pie
menu includes the interaction "Tease."

See? We just had a social interaction. Life is
indeed very much like *The Sims.*

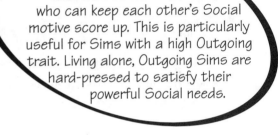

TIP

Start each new house-
hold with at least two Sims
who can keep each other's Social
motive score up. This is particularly
useful for Sims with a high Outgoing
trait. Living alone, Outgoing Sims are
hard-pressed to satisfy their
powerful Social needs.

The Relationship Score

Good relationships are important to a Sim's
ongoing struggle to get ahead. One primary
objective in *The Sims* is to raise Relationship
scores past the 50-point mark (the "friendship
threshhold") with as many Sim neighbors as
possible. The more friends you make, the
higher you can climb on your career ladder.

**Fig. 5-1. Here, Bob Weigel needs more family friends.
Work on getting his relationships with people outside
the family above 50 points.**

Sure, it's fun to slap folks. Slapping, teasing, bragging, scaring, insulting—you can
indulge your dark side freely in *The Sims,* too. What a great game! But of course, you
won't make many friends that way. Real life is like that too, I think.

For more about friends and careers (and a list of how many friends you need for each
job promotion), refer to "Careers and Skills." For now, though, let's just say friends in
The Sims are more than just friends. They're rungs in the career ladder.

Daily Relationship Decay

Relationships decay 2 points on both sides every day, whether the other Sim lives in your
house or not. When a Sim's Relationship score with a friend falls close to 50, the friend
calls to say, "We need to see each other more often."

Tips from the Testers

When trying to build friendships, avoid letting Sims choose their own social interactions with other Sims. They often make horrible decisions. The best way to build a good relationship with another Sim quickly: talk until the Relationship score hits 30. Compliment until 60. Hug until 100.

Avoid activating the "love bit," however. Don't kiss other Sims unless you're really looking for a mate. Love can slow the friend-making process because it provokes jealousy. Just make friends and send them on their way.

—Andrew Blomquist, Tester

Influence of Mood and Personality

A Sim's Playful, Nice, and Outgoing personality settings influence the interactions they choose. Consult the astrological signs for clues about which Sims get along and which will clash. (For more on this, see "Personality.") Sims in a bad mood, however, are very likely to have negative social interactions regardless of their personality traits. If either Sim engaged in a one-on-one social interaction—talking, joking, and so on—is in a bad mood, that interaction is more likely to have a negative outcome.

Topics of Conversation

Talk interests are ingrained. Different Sims have different interests. There is one exception to this rule, however. Adults will "map" their talk topics to match that of the kids topics. For more on this, read on about Kids/Adult Conversations. Sims with similar interests are likely to have very rewarding conversations. Keep an eye on the topic icons that appear in the talk bubbles above the heads of conversing Sims. Keep track of which neighbors share common interests.

Fig. 5-2. Keep an eye on those talk bubbles above Sims' heads. They reveal topics of interest and disinterest.

NOTE

Unless they're talking while they do something else (such as watching TV or eating—see "Group Talk" later in this section), Sims can talk to each other only one-on-one.

There are 12 general conversation topics in *The Sims*. Four are adult-only, four are kid-only, and four are available to both kids and adults. Every Sim has a high, medium, or low interest level (based on a scale of 1 to 10) in each conversation topic. These interest levels are assigned arbitrarily when a character is created and they never change.

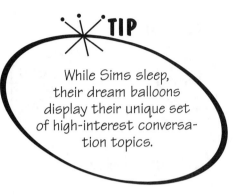

TIP

While Sims sleep, their dream balloons display their unique set of high-interest conversation topics.

The Conversation Icons

Again, there are specific topics for adults and kids, as well as topics shared by both. Each conversation topic has three icons to represent it.

Adult-Only Topics

Money

Travel

Politics

'60s Stuff

Kid-Only Topics

Toys

Aliens

Pets

School

Adult/Kid Topics

Weather

Sports

Music

Outdoors

How Sim Conversations Work

The person who initiates a conversation always leads with a high-interest topic. A conversation is capped at four back-and-forth volleys of talk, but may end before that point due to low interest. Whether the conversation continues depends on each listener's interest level in the topic being discussed:

- A listener with high interest in the previous topic will continue talking about it.

- An even chance exists that a listener with medium interest in the previous topic will either continue discussing the same topic or change the subject.

- A 10 percent chance exists that a listener with low interest in the previous topic will continue on the same topic, a 40 percent chance the listener will change subjects, and a 50 percent chance the listener will exit the conversation.

A listener with a high interest in the topic will randomly display one of the topic's three icons. A listener with low interest in the topic, or one who changes the subject, will displays an X balloon—a talk balloon showing the topic's icon with an X through it.

Fig. 5-3. This conversation got off on the wrong foot. Bob led with a remark about Flower Power in the '60s. But despite his hippie appearance, Biff isn't interested in the topic.

How Conversations Are Scored

There is a Relationship effect and a Social motive effect for the listener in each talk volley. A listener who likes the topic gets 5 Social points and 3 Relationship points. A listener who dislikes the topic gets 3 Social points and -3 Relationship points. In other words, even low interest can raise a Sim's Social motive in a Talk interaction.

Kid/Adult Conversations

Kids starting a conversation with an adult will bring up a kid-only or shared topic. Kids don't talk about adult topics, *ever.* Adults starting a conversation with a kid will bring up a kid-only or shared topic, as well. In this case, adult topics "map" to kid topics. That is, the adult's interest level in one of his or her own topics is applied to the kid topic.

Adult topics map to kid topics as follows:

ADULT TOPIC	CORRESPONDING KID TOPIC
Travel	Toys
Money	Aliens
Politics	Pets
'60s	School

Group Talk

When Sims talk while doing something else (such as watching TV or eating), they run a different kind of conversation algorithm, called Group Talk. The Sims take turns speaking about something of high interest to the speaker. (This is a good way to find out visitors' interests.) A speaking Sim gets 8 Social points and 1 Relationship point toward one Sim motive in the group.

Fig. 5-4. Group activities that offer Group Talk opportunities are classic "win-win" situations. Everybody gets positive Social and Relationship points, regardless of interests or personal feelings toward other participants.

Fig. 5-5. Some Group Talk objects (such as the §6,500 hot tub) are expensive. But a simple meal together triggers Group Talk, too.

> **NOTE**
> Group Talk uses only the four shared (adult/kid) topics—Weather, Sports, Music, and Outdoors.

In Group Talk, Sims may disagree but there is no relationship loss. They also don't have to worry about matching topics with each other. (They'll only discuss Kid/Adult topics, never Kid-only or Adult-only topics.) Thus, group activities present nice, safe ways to boost Social and Relationship scores without risking negative interaction. (See the corresponding tip from tester Syruss Flyte.)

Group Activities with Group Talk

Sims who join in the following activities take turns speaking to the group. Each speaker gains 8 Social points and adds 1 Relationship point toward each participant:

- Eat group meal
- Watch TV
- Hot tub
- Chessboard
- Large train set
- Dollhouse
- Pinball
- Pool table

Group Activities with No Group Talk

Some group activities don't feature Group Talk, with its automatic increase in Social and Relationship points. That doesn't mean such boosts aren't possible. In some cases, the activity offers random increases to your Sim's Social motive and/or Relationship score toward other participants.

Fig. 5-6. Dancing at the stereo is fun, AND it guarantees random group talk Social/Relationship gains.

- **Basketball Hoop:** Random Social/ Relationship gain
- **Piano:** Watchers gain Relationship points toward player based on player's Creativity skill. Higher skill means more points gained.
- **Stereo (Dance):** Random Social/ Relationship gain.
- **Play Structure:** No Social/Relationship gain
- **Swimming Pool:** No Social/Relationship gain

Tips From the Testers

Sims with different sets of interests may find it hard to develop friendships, but Group Talk situations eliminate negative interactions. Use them to boost Relationship scores between incompatible Sims.

Prepare a group meal and eat, watch TV, crank up the model railroad set, play chess. Best of all, *use that hot tub!* When other Sims join the activity, your Sim's relationship with them goes up without any of the trouble that can come with regular social interactions.

—Syruss Flyte, Tester

Social Outcomes

A number of factors can influence social outcomes. In this section, we examine these factors, and include a point table that shows exactly how each potential outcome affects Social and Relationship scores. But first, let's talk about how to resurrect a deteriorating social life, and then take a quick peek at a couple of special social interactions that can trigger far-reaching outcomes.

When Social Life Goes Sour: How to Avoid the Downward Spiral

Most social interactions have more than one possible outcome. Mood, Motive levels, personality type, Relationship scores, and other factors influence that outcome. In turn, the outcome (good, bad, or indifferent) affects Social and Relationship scores, those twin indicators of social health.

Thus, if things start going bad, your Sim can get caught in a downward social spiral. Bad scores trigger bad interactions, which in turn send scores south still further. In fact, it can be very, very difficult to salvage

Fig. 5-7. If your Social/Relationship scores are buried in the red, load up on objects that offer Group Talk interactions.

any relationship, much less a bad one, with your Social score mired in the red. Here's our advice on escaping this trap.

First, fill your house with group activity objects that trigger the automatic Group Talk interaction. (See "Group Talk. ") Again, Group Talk situations eliminate negative interactions. Even Sims that hate you will get a positive social buzz from a soak in the hot tub.

Second, avoid one-on-one interactions with other Sims until you've raised your Social score to at least 0, preferably higher. After that, limit your social choices to Talk. Talking may trigger negative outcomes, but the risk is minimized. Keep talking and arranging Group Talk activities until your Social and Relationship scores climb back into a good green range.

Jealousy

Jealousy is a bad thing. It slaughters the Social motive, big time. Let's say Sim Betty loves Sim Bob. Both are in the same room. If Sim Jezebel enters and tries to engage in a dicey interaction (listed below) with Bob, Betty will get jealous.

If Betty gets jealous, look out. She crosses her arms for a moment. Her Social score drops like a rock. Then she'll likely slap the snot out of Jezebel, flushing the harlot's Social scores right down the tubes, too.

The four interactions that can induce jealousy are:

- Kiss
- Hug
- Flirt
- Give Backrub

Attack

Sims can be vicious, given certain circumstances. A jealous or grouchy Sim can make manifest dark feelings by attacking another

Fig. 5-8. Jealousy decimates a Sim's Social motive score. Plus it triggers bad social interactions...like this impending slapfest, for example.

Fig. 5-9. Careful! Attacks between family members can drive the loser out of the game.

Sim. Dust flies, smoke clears, and there's the loser, humiliated on the floor, with the winner crowing above.

Fortunately, strict rules govern this sort of Neanderthal behavior. Adults can attack other adults, but never kids. Kids can attack other kids, but not adults. Fights are moderated by the Nice personality trait. A very nice Sim will almost never attack, while a not-so-nice Sim (one with a Nice score of zero) is much more likely to. Adults might decide to move out of the house if attacked by a family member (25 percent chance), but kids won't. Any visitor who ends up on the losing end of an attack will leave the house immediately.

Limits to Social Interaction

Not all interactions are available for all Sim types. Kids, in particular, can't engage in actions such as Kiss, Flirt, Compliment, and Slap. Adults, on the other hand, can't play Tag, doggone it. The following tables lists the possible combinations.

POSSIBLE ADULT/CHILD INTERACTIONS

INTERACTION	ADULT TO ADULT	KID TO KID	ADULT TO KID	KID TO ADULT
Kiss	X	—	—	—
Hug	X	X	X	X
Flirt	X	—	—	—
Give Backrub	X	—	—	—
Compliment	X	—	—	—
Cheer Up	X	X	X	X
Dance	X	—	—	—
Entertain	X	X	X	X
Give Gift	X	X	X	X
Joke	X	X	X	X
Talk	X	X	X	X
Call Here	X	X	X	X
Tickle	X	X	X	X
Brag	X	X	X	X
Insult	X	X	X	X
Slap	X	—	—	—
Scare	X	X	X	X
Tease	X	X	X	X
Attack	X	X	—	—
Apologize	X	—	—	—
Tag	—	X	—	—
Say Goodbye	X	X	X	—

Factors that Influence Social Outcomes

Every social interaction carries "baggage." When a Sim talks to another Sim, the outcome of is affected by age (adult or child), sex, mood, individual personality traits, and other aspects of their relationship. Are they friends? Are they in love? Are their Social needs high or low?

All these things influence available pie menu choices and the outcome of selected interactions. In the table below, we list the factors that influence the outcome of various types of social interaction.

```
rel = Relationship
out = Outgoing
play = Playful
ff = friend flag
ss = same sex
rom = romance flag
age = adult/child
social = Social motive value
vis = visitor
budget = household budget
nice = Nice
body = Body
```

SOCIAL OUTCOME FACTORS

INTERACTION	FACTORS THAT DETERMINE APPEARANCE ON MENU	FACTORS THAT DETERMINE OUTCOME
Cheer Up	ff, mood (of friend), nice	rel
Kiss	ss, mood, rel, age	rel, mood, ss
Dance	age, mood, out, rel	rel, out, mood
Backrub	age, nice, mood, rel, out, ss	rel, out, ss
Flirt	age, social, ss, out, mood, rel, rom	rel, mood, ss
Gift	vis, budget, nice, mood, rel	rel, mood
Hug	age, out, mood, rel, ss	rel, out, mood, ss
Entertain	social, out, play, mood, rel	play, rel
Compliment	age, nice, out, mood, rel	rel, mood
Joke	play, mood, rel	play, mood, rel
Talk	mood, rel, out	topics match

INTERACTION	FACTORS THAT DETERMINE APPEARANCE ON MENU	FACTORS THAT DETERMINE OUTCOME
Brag	nice, out, social, rel	rel, mood
Tease	nice, mood, rel	rel, mood
Tickle	social, out, play, active, mood, rel	rel, play
Insult	nice, mood, rel	nice
Slap	age, nice, mood, rel	nice, mood
Apologize	rel	mood
Scare	nice, mood, play, rel	play, mood
Attack	age, nice, mood, rel	body

How Social Interactions Are Scored

We've talked about how various factors can affect the outcomes of social interactions. Once those outcomes are triggered, your Sim's Social and Relationship scores change. Naturally, different outcomes have different effects on these scores.

The table that follows illustrates how each outcome of each possible social interaction affects Relationship and Social scores. In general, note that social interactions rarely have a negative effect on the Social motive. Bad outcomes usually score 0 Social points, at worst, and can even result in positive Social points. Apparently, bad social contact is better than no contact at all.

> NOTE
>
> In the following table, "Relationship Change" refers to the change in score toward the Sim's partner in the listed interaction.

EFFECTS OF OUTCOMES ON SOCIAL/RELATIONSHIP SCORES FOR INITIATOR AND RECEIVER

INTERACTION	RESPONSE	RELATIONSHIP CHANGE	SOCIAL SCORE CHANGE
Attack	Win Fight	-5	10
Attack	Lose Fight	-10	-20
Give Back Rub	Good	5	7
Give Back Rub	Bad	-7	0
Receive Back Rub	Good	9	13
Receive Back Rub	Bad	-10	0
Cheer Up	Good	5	7
Cheer Up	Neutral	0	5
Cheer Up	Bad	-3	0

EFFECTS OF OUTCOMES ON SOCIAL/RELATIONSHIP SCORES FOR INITIATOR AND RECEIVER, continued

INTERACTION	RESPONSE	RELATIONSHIP CHANGE	SOCIAL SCORE CHANGE
Be Cheered Up	Good	10	10
Be Cheered Up	Neutral	0	5
Be Cheered Up	Bad	-10	0
Hug	Good	7	15
Hug	Tentative	2	7
Hug	Refuse	-10	0
Be Hugged	Good	8	15
Be Hugged	Tentative	4	7
Be Hugged	Refuse	-10	0
Flirt	Good	5	13
Flirt	Ignore	-5	0
Flirt	Refuse	-10	-17
Be Flirted With	Good	10	13
Be Flirted With	Ignore	0	0
Be Flirted With	Refuse	-10	0
Compliment	Accept	5	5
Compliment	Reject	-10	0
Be Complimented	Accept	5	11
Be Complimented	Reject	-7	0
Give Gift	Accept	5	7
Give Gift	Stomp	-15	0
Receive Gift	Accept	10	13
Receive Gift	Stomp	-5	0
Insult	Cry	5	0
Insult	Stoic	0	3
Insult	Angry	-10	7
Be Insulted	Cry	-12	-13
Be Insulted	Stoic	-5	-5
Be Insulted	Angry	-14	-7
Slap	Cry	0	3

INTERACTION	RESPONSE	RELATIONSHIP CHANGE	SOCIAL SCORE CHANGE
Slap	Slap Back	-10	-7
Be Slapped	Cry	-20	-17
Be Slapped	Slap Back	-15	7
Tease	Giggle	5	7
Tease	Cry	-4	0
Be Teased	Giggle	5	7
Be Teased	Cry	-13	-7
Scare	Laugh	5	10
Scare	Angry	-5	0
Be Scared	Laugh	5	8
Be Scared	Angry	-10	0
Talk	High Interest Topic	3	5
Talk	Like Topic	3	5
Talk	Dislike Topic	-3	3
Talk	Hate Topic	-3	3
Group Talk	N/A	1	8
Dance	Accept	8	13
Dance	Refuse	-5	0
Be Danced With	Accept	10	13
Be Danced With	Refuse	-5	0
Tickle	Accept	5	13
Tickle	Refuse	-5	0
Be Tickled	Accept	8	13
Be Tickled	Refuse	-8	0
Brag	Good	5	13
Brag	Bad	-5	0
Be Bragged To	Good	5	7
Be Bragged To	Bad	-5	0
Joke	Laugh	5	13
Joke	Giggle	2	7
Joke	Uninterested	-6	0
Listen to Joke	Laugh	7	13
Listen to Joke	Giggle	3	7

EFFECTS OF OUTCOMES ON SOCIAL/RELATIONSHIP SCORES FOR INITIATOR AND RECEIVER, continued

INTERACTION	RESPONSE	RELATIONSHIP CHANGE	SOCIAL SCORE CHANGE
Listen to Joke	Uninterested	-7	0
Entertain	Laugh	4	7
Entertain	Boo	-15	0
Be Entertained	Laugh	8	13
Be Entertained	Boo	-7	0
Apologize	Accept	10	15
Apologize	Reject	-10	0
Be Apologized To	Accept	10	15
Be Apologized To	Reject	-10	0
Kiss	Passion	12	20
Kiss	Polite	5	10
Kiss	Deny	-15	5
Be Kissed	Passion	12	20
Be Kissed	Polite	5	10
Be Kissed	Deny	-10	0

Friendship

Friendship is a key state in *The Sims*. Job advancement is impossible without building a network of neighborhood friends. (See "Careers" for details on this.) Two Sims don't become "friends" until both have a relationship to each other of at least 50. When this happens, you see that little blue smiley face appear below each other's picture in the Relationships subpanel and above their heads on the game screen.

Fig. 5-10. One of your biggest goals in THE SIMS is to grow the number circled here—your Family Friend Count. With only two friends, this family has a lot of work to do.

NOTE
The key number in a friendship is 50. To be friends, each Sim must have a 50 Relationship score with the other. If either score drops below 50, the friendship ends.

Friendships are two-way streets, though. If the relationship of either Sim toward the other drops below 50, the blue face disappears and the friendship ends—at least, until you repair it with some good socializing. Fortunately, friends warn you via phone call when their score falls near 50.

TIP

Remember, the decay rate for all Relationship scores is 2 points per day. If Sims don't spend regular time with a friend, the relationship will eventually fade below the friendship threshold.

The Romance Bit

Unlike real-life love, where everything is *always perfectly equal,* romance in *The Sims* can be one-sided. If your Sim develops at least a 70 Relationship with another Sim, and then performs a "romantic interaction" (Hug, Kiss, Flirt, Give Backrub) with him or her, your Sim will likely fall in love. Or, in programmer-speak, "their romance bit will get set." Only then will the pie menu give your Sim the choice to Propose.

Remember, though—unlike friendship, love can be a one-way transaction.

Propose/Move In

Flowchart time! Will Wright handed us the following chart below scribbled in pencil on ugly graph paper. It describes how *The Sims* processes the act of proposing to a prospective mate. Marketing studies, however, indicate that

Fig. 5-11. Ah, romance. Raise the relationship with your love-target above 70, try a few romantic interactions—Hug, Backrub, Flirt, Kiss—and sooner or later you'll score a heart.

TIP

Love can be lucrative! A good strategy for quickly increasing funds is to persuade neighbors who live alone to marry you or move in. If they say yes, their net worth is added to yours.

consumers buy strategy guides almost entirely based on the aesthetic beauty of flow charts. So we took Will's pathetic scribble, digitally enhanced it, and then added immeasurable graphic nuance. Now buy this book.

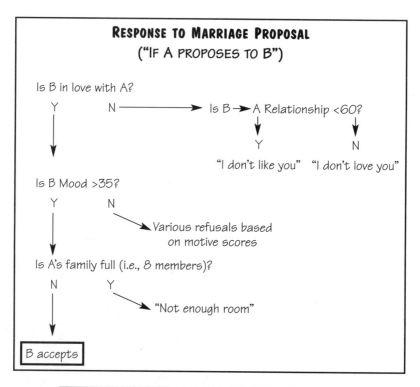

RESPONSE TO MARRIAGE PROPOSAL
("IF A PROPOSES TO B")

Is B in love with A?

Y   N ──────────────────► Is B ➤ A Relationship <60?

                                          Y   N

                                  "I don't like you"   "I don't love you"

Is B Mood >35?

Y   N
                    ↘ Various refusals based
                         on motive scores

Is A's family full (i.e., 8 members)?

N   Y
                    ↘ "Not enough room"

B accepts

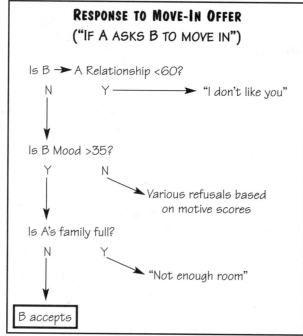

RESPONSE TO MOVE-IN OFFER
("IF A ASKS B TO MOVE IN")

Is B ➤ A Relationship <60?

N   Y ──────────────────► "I don't like you"

Is B Mood >35?

Y   N
                    ↘ Various refusals based
                         on motive scores

Is A's family full?

N   Y
                    ↘ "Not enough room"

B accepts

Weddings

The nuptial ceremony takes place automatically when a one Sim accepts another's marriage proposal. Don't blink. It happens pretty fast. Then the new spouse brings a job and income into the household. If the spouse was the only adult in the previous home, the new partner brings his or her net worth…and kids, if any. (This leaves the ex-house empty and up for sale.) Interestingly, if a marrying Sim has kids, and another adult (a suffering ex-spouse, perhaps) remains in the old house, the kids stay put. Hey, it's only fair. Didn't you ever read *Horton Hatches the Egg?*

Fig. 5-12. OK, it sounds crass, but the best thing about weddings is the additional income a marriage brings into your household. Now you can buy some REALLY good stuff!

Family and Housemates

Family can be the warm, cozy hearth of *The Sims*. If you create Sim families with nice, outgoing personalities and guide them into similar schedules—eating and watching TV at the same time, for example—then families can do a pretty good job of taking care of their own social needs without micromanagement.

Tips from the Testers

A two-member family is the best way to keep up your Sims' Social motive score. Add a third member to manage household chores and procure friends so your other two Sims can focus on skill-building and maintaining a positive mood.

—Ed O'Tey, Tester

Sleeping with Housemates

Just because two Sims live together doesn't mean they like each other well enough to share a bed. If Sims won't sleep together, you'll have to improve their relationship to the Friendship level (50 points or higher) to get them both sleeping in the same bed at the same time. This doesn't apply to children, however. Children can sleep with a fellow household adult or child regardless of Relationship scores. Sims don't have to be of different genders or in love to share a bed. But they do have to be friends.

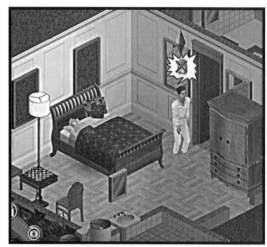

Fig. 5-13. This man won't sleep with that woman in the bed because they're not "friends." Know many guys like that?

Babies

Whenever two household members of the opposite sex kiss with passion, they trigger a 1 in 5 chance the game will offer them a baby. (We're glad the process is a bit more complicated in real life.) Note that there is also a chance that you'll get the option of adopting a baby. If there are two adults in love in a house, there's a random chance of getting an offer to adopt over the phone. If you choose to accept, the little bundle of joy appears in its crib, ready to be fed, played with, and sung to for three days. (Changing diapers, thankfully, isn't an option.) The baby's gender is randomly assigned, and its personality based on the parents' personality.

Fig. 5-14. Baby demands can wreak havoc on a household for the three days of their Sim infancy. Keep babies fed and sing them to sleep to minimize the time crunch.

TIP

Two-parent households can take turns staying home from work to care for the baby. That way no one will lose their job.

After three days, the baby morphs into a full-grown kid.

You can move cribs, but you can't delete them. Sims don't autonomously care for (Feed or Sing To) a baby. But they will choose to play with it. Both family members and visitors can interact with the baby, which is a "special object" with just two motives—Hunger and Energy. As these motives decrease, the baby cries. Crying babies wake up sleeping adults (but not kids) in the same room.

The Baby Ratings

Each of the baby motives—Hunger and Energy—has a rating from 0 to 2. Each motive decreases by 1 every two hours, except when the baby is sleeping. Playing with or singing to a baby raises its Energy score; feeding raises its Hunger score. (Duh!)

- 2 Energy/Hunger means the baby is fully rested/fed and doesn't cry.
- 1 Energy/Hunger means the baby is slightly tired/hungry and snuffles a small cry.
- 0 Energy/Hunger score means the baby desperately needs to sleep/eat. Baby makes a shrill, insistent cry.

Sleeping Babies

Sim babies can sleep only when their Hunger rating is above 0. Once asleep, a baby continues sleeping for six hours. While the baby sleeps, its Hunger score won't drop below 1; Hunger can fall below 1 only after baby wakes up. Sleeping returns Energy level to 2.

TIP

Your primary baby-care goal: *Get them to sleep!* Otherwise, he or she requires constant care. Yes, playing with baby might be fun, but it's also very time-consuming.

Interacting with Babies

If a baby is quiet, you know both its needs are satisfied. But if a baby cries, you can't be sure whether Hunger or Energy is low. Best bet: feed the baby first. If Hunger reaches 0 while you playfully bounce the baby like an idiot, you risk losing the baby to Child Protective Services. (More on this in a minute.)

TIP

If a baby continues crying during the interaction you've chosen, your choice isn't raising the baby's low motive. Remember, babies have only two needs. Try an interaction to satisfy the other need.

If the baby cries quietly, one or both of the motives must be at 1 (and no lower). Feed the baby first. If the crying doesn't stop, you know the Energy rating must be at 1. Now choose Sing. Singing puts the baby to sleep for six hours, which raises Energy to 2. (Choosing Play also raises Energy to 2, but it keeps the baby awake, which means its motives drop again in just two hours.)

A shrill cry tells you one of the baby's motives is at 0. Feed it first—and hurry! If that doesn't work, the baby's Energy must be at 0. Playing has no effect on an over-tired baby. Only singing works. Again, the Sing interaction puts the baby to sleep for six hours, returning its Energy to 2.

Losing Babies

If baby's Hunger rating goes to 0 for more than 60 Sim-minutes—well, sorry, this is a failure state, and you win the Joan Crawford "Mommy Dearest" Award. An unflappable Social Worker arrives and takes the baby. This sad episode can happen anytime (day or night) during the three-day babyhood period.

Kids

If a baby survives for three days after birth, he or she breaks out of the crib, stretches, and becomes a full-fledged, fun-loving Sim kid. Of course, you can add kids to your

Fig. 5-15. This Social Worker means business. If you don't want to lose your baby, keep it fed.

household right from the start in the Create a Family screen. Either way, you now face a daunting new challenge—Parenthood.

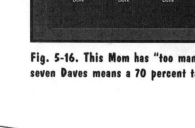

Fig. 5-16. This Mom has "too many Daves." But hey, seven Daves means a 70 percent tax cut.

NOTE
Kids can save you money. You get a 10 percent "tax credit" on bills for each child in the household.

Attributes: Baby-to-Kid

A kid is a fully functioning Sim, with all eight motives working and a full set of talk interests. If you crafted your own kid at the Create a Sim screen, you allocated personality traits and *The Sims* assigned a random set of talk interests. But what happens if a kid comes into the world via babyhood?

Oddly, a Sim child "inherits" traits and interests from either mother or father, or from an average of both parents. Who would think up a cockamamie system like that? Skills are preset to a random amount; kids can't increase skills during the game. Kid skill values determine only how well they play piano, paint, or play basketball.

Kids and School

If a kid misses a day of school, his or her Report Card grade drops a whole grade point—for example, from B+ to C+. Kids can bring grades up by going to school in a good mood, or by selecting Study for School at a bookshelf or computer. If a Sim child's grade drops to F and stays there for three days, the kid must go to Military School. If that happens, the family account is charged a one-time fee of §1,000. Ouch! Worse, your deadbeat kid leaves the household and disappears into SimSpace, never to return.

Kids and Social Interactions

See the preceding Possible Adult/Child Interactions table shows which interactions are available to Sim kids. As you might expect, kids are limited in their object interactions, as well. No stiff drinks at the bar. No cooking or lighting fires.

NOTE
Fun matters more to kids. It plays a bigger part in their mood and drains quickly. So kids have to do fun stuff a lot.

Visitors

Visitors are neighbors. And neighbors, unless you import families or keep the Newbies and Goths, are Sims *you* created and placed in the neighborhood. Keep that in mind if they exasperate *The Sims* in your current household. It's your fault.

TIP

Always keep a group platter of food available for neighbors who drop by. First thing home from work—hit the fridge and Serve Dinner. Then take care of basic needs, such as Bladder or Hygiene, to be in the best mood possible when visitors arrive.

Visitor Motives and Intelligence

Actually, visitors are somewhat "smarter" than your current family members. That is, they take care of their own needs better. When presented with choices, visitors always pick the interaction with the highest happiness contribution value (the one that will improve their mood the most).

But neighbors are polite. They won't raid your fridge if they're hungry, for example, or shoot a game of pool without an invitation. Instead, they go home. So if you want to keep your visitors around long enough to make friends, you must provide them with opportunities to satisfy certain needs. (See "Keeping Neighbors Happy.")

TIP

Buy a phone immediately! A phone allows Sims to invite visitors and order services. But your Sims can call only folks they've already met, so be sure to greet neighbors when they drop by.

Fig. 5-17. Keep a platter of food on the table for visitors. They often arrive hungry.

Greeting Visitors

Each neighbor has an equal likelihood of visiting. Visitors ring the doorbell and wait to be greeted. If one of your family Sims doesn't greet the visitor within one Sim-hour, they stroll back home. Your most interruptible family member (that is, anyone idling) will answer the door; only one family member greets the visitor.

Fig. 5-18. Sim visitors are remarkably patient, waiting an entire Sim-hour for you to answer the doorbell. If you don't greet them within that time, they head back home.

The type of greeting depends on your Sim's relationship to the visitor. If they're in love with each other, they exchange a "polite" kiss. If they're friends, they hug briefly. In all other cases, they shake hands. Greeted visitors can move freely through the doorway and wander through the house.

Neighbor Visit Schedule

Neighbors in *The Sims* are very, you know, *neighborly*. They like to drop by, see how you're doing, check out your stuff—er, your state of mind. And they do it with almost frightening regularity.

The Welcome Wagon

If neighbors exist on Sim Lane, one or two will drop by at 9:30 a.m. on the first day. *The Sims* does this to help jump-start your social life. Game designers can be so darned thoughtful.

Drop-Ins

If there are neighbors you haven't met, *The Sims* will sort through them each day at noon and 6 p.m. and decide whether to send one to visit you in "drop-in" fashion. Drop-ins come unannounced to your door. The more full houses in the neighborhood, the more likely the game will find someone to drop in on you.

Once you greet neighbors, however, they can no longer be selected to drop in. You must call neighbors you've met already to arrange visits.

Daily Walk-by

Sometimes your Sims can't greet drop-in visitors because they're at work or busy. But neighbors take daily walks around the Sim Lane block. At 10 a.m., 2 p.m., 4 p.m., and 8 p.m., the game selects a random neighbor to stroll the sidewalk past your house. These strollers walk directly off the lot unless one of your family members greets them first. You must direct this greeting, however. Family members never greet strolling neighbors autonomously.

Fig. 5-19. If you're having trouble meeting people, hang out on the sidewalk and intercept strollers. Neighbors walk by daily at 10 a.m., 2 p.m., 4 p.m., and 8 p.m..

Calling Neighbors

First of all, in a grand concession to reality, *The Sims* makes it impossible to call neighbors *who don't have a phone*. As *The Sims* manual points out a number of times, put a phone into every house before you do anything else. Without phones, Sims are hard to reach. Impossible, in fact.

Neighbors are more likely to respond positively to a phone invitation if they like the Sim who invites them (it's irrelevant how the caller feels). A neighbor who accepts an invitation has a 25 percent chance of asking permission to bring friends. (This is an option only if the neighbor actually *has* friends—that is, Sims with whom they have a 50 or higher Relationship score.) If you say yes, the neighbor may bring along as many as three more Sims.

If you call neighbors between 1 and 6 a.m., they won't come over. No surprise there. If fact, they get real ornery and your Relationship with them decreases. If you call any Sim with whom your Relationship is under 50 they'll hang up on you. Finally, all Sim kids wisely refuse invitations after 7:30 p.m., no matter what.

> NOTE
> Sims don't hide their feelings well. When a Sim calls a neighbor, voices on either end of the phone reflect the quality of the relationship.

Start Motives and Leave Conditions

When visitors arrive, their motives start out at the following values. For those with a range, the start value is randomly selected from within the range.

VISITOR'S STARTING MOTIVES

MOTIVE	STARTING VALUE
Bladder	0–30
Comfort	30–70
Energy	35
Fun	-20–20
Hunger	-30--20
Hygiene	90
Social	-50--40

Visitors go back home when the time passes 1 a.m. or any one of their motives falls below the critical values in the following table. If the latter happens, the exiting Sims' thought balloons indicate which motive caused them to leave.

VISITORS WILL LEAVE...

IF MOTIVE:	DROPS BELOW VALUE:
Energy	-80
Comfort	-70
Hunger	-50
Hygiene	-70
Bladder	-90
Social	-85
Fun	-55
Room	-100
Mood	-75

Keeping Visitors Happy

Yes, visitors are smart. If you give them good choices, they tend to make good decisions. But it's up to you to be a good host. Sure, talking is important to raise Social and Relationship scores. But if you focus on social interactions only, your visitors will

Fig. 5-20. Visitors arrive with their motive levels fairly low. Best be ready with activities to meet their needs—have the TV on, the food out, and so forth.

leave when other motives fall below their critical values.

Keep group platters of food on the table for Hunger. For Fun, keep the TV and stereo blasting; hit the hot tub or pool to invite followers. Also important—let your guests wander off to do their own thing at times. They need to sit down and relax for Comfort, or use the bathroom for Bladder and Hygiene purposes.

Activities Available to Visitors

Not all activities in your home are available to neighbors. Note three types:

Family Member–Enabled Activities

One of your family members must "prepare" these two interactions before a neighbor can partake. First, neighbors can't help themselves to food in the fridge. They can eat only a prepared meal. So before guests arrive, click on the fridge and Serve Dinner (or any meal appropriate to the time of day). Second, neighbors won't turn on your TV. So turn it on for them. Once you do, they can sit and watch.

Joinable Activities

Neighbors won't perform certain interactions until a family member does them first. A Sim who starts an activity can invite the visitor to join. (Just click on the visitor and select Join or its equivalent.) Neighbors can join these activities autonomously, if they need the motives offered.

JOINABLE ACTIVITIES

AFTER "HOST" SIM USES OBJECT	ACTIVITY AVAILABLE TO VISITORS
Basketball Hoop	Join
Chess	Join
Dollhouse	Watch
Hot Tub	Join
Pinball Machine	Join
Play Structure	Join
Piano	Watch
Pool Table	Join
Stereo	Join Dance
Train Set	Watch

Autonomous Activities

Neighbors can take care of their own needs, in many cases. The basic strategy: don't hog all their time. Give visitors a chance to grab a cup of coffee, use the toilet, or sit on the couch if they need it. Here's a list of the activities a visitor will engage in autonomously if left alone long enough to do so.

VISITORS' AUTONOMOUS ACTIVITIES

OBJECT	AUTONOMOUS ACTION
Aquarium	Watch Fish
Baby	Play
Bar	Have a drink
Chair	Sit
Chair (Recliner)	Sit
Coffee (Espresso Machine)	Drink Espresso

OBJECT	AUTONOMOUS ACTION
Coffeemaker	Drink Coffee
Fire	Panic
Flamingo	View
Fountain	Play
Lava Lamp	View
Painting	View
Pool	Swim
Pool Diving Board	Dive In
Pool Ladder	Get In/Out
Sculpture	View
Sink	Wash Hands
Sofa	Sit
Toilet	Use, Flush
Tombstone/Urn	Mourn
Toy Box	Play
Trash Can (Inside)	Dispose

TIP

Give guests freedom to make some autonomous decisions. But always find time to interact with them, too. If you don't, visitors feel ignored and head home.

Ghosts!

Sims can die. That's bad. If they die on your property, they create an urn (inside the house) or tombstone (outside the house). But departed Sims don't consider urns or tombstones to be sufficient memorials. In fact, they want to keep their icy fingers in your business.

So every night at 11pm, every urn and tombstone on your lot has a 1 in 8 chance of spewing out the ghost of the dead Sim buried there! Then they come haunt your house. Cool!

Fig. 5-21. Sims who die on your lot aren't completely gone. Each tombstone or urn can produce the spirit of the dearly departed at 11 o'clock each night.

How Ghosts Operate

Each ghost is a pale version of its predeath self. However, ghosts are invisible much of the time. They glide around the house making a haunting, ghostly sound. This is amusing, but it has a downside. The moaning wakes up adults (but not kids) sleeping in the same room. So it's really bad for healthy sleep patterns.

If a Sim is awake when the ghost enters the room, things get even more fun. The ghost remains invisible until it slips behind the person. Then it suddenly becomes visible and scares the poor Sim. The scared Sim's reaction is to panic and run away. Fun! If more than two Sims are awake in the room, the ghost will scare the closest. If no one in the room is awake, the ghost will wander around sadly for a while, and then disappear.

Tips from the Testers

Ghosts won't climb stairs! If you have a two-story house, put your Sims' bedrooms on the second floor and keep urns on the ground floor. This keeps ghosts from awakening your Sims in the middle of the night.

—Syruss Flyte, Tester

Getting Rid of Ghosts

Ghosts are amusing. But, again, they can be annoying, too. Fortunately, they're pretty easy to exorcise. Ghosts are deleted if you delete their urn/tombstone or bulldoze the lot. If an urn is among the objects in a house a family is evicted from, it gets sold with the rest of the stuff. However, if a tombstone is in the yard when a family is evicted, the tombstone remains (as if it were an architectural object).

6
Careers and Skills

D eadbeat families don't last long in *The Sims*. Oh, they may draw a lucky "chance card" here and there to keep them alive a few more weeks. But sooner or later the food runs out. Burial urns appear. Fortunately, jobs are easy to get, and career advancement is a large part of the fun in *The Sims*. It's an invigorating challenge to follow a career track to the top, make big bucks, and then buy a Large Black Slab for §12,648.

In this section we examine the game's career tracks and offer tips on job advancement. We go on to cover skill-building, the key to getting ahead in any career. A comprehensive table at the end lists requirements and benefits for the 10 positions within each of the game's 10 career tracks.

Careers

As you read in the game manual, *The Sims* features 10 fabulous career tracks—Business, Entertainment, Law Enforcement, Life of Crime, Medicine, Military, Politics, Pro Athlete, Science, and Xtreme. Each track has 10 positions, starting with low-paying flunky jobs, such as Waiter and Team Mascot, and building up to top-level glamour gigs, such as Business Tycoon or Criminal Mastermind.

The tables in the section "The 10 Career Tracks" provide a complete listing of salaries, work hours, skill requirements, and other information for every job in *The Sims*.

NOTE
Sims who change career tracks must start their new tracks at entry level. However, they keep all the skill points they've earned. Thus, job promotions in the new track happen faster if they're already skilled in the right areas.

Choosing a Career Track

As we pointed out earlier, having certain personality traits makes it easier to build certain skills. Therefore, the job you choose for each Sim should emphasize skills the Sim's personality will enhance.

NOTE
Careers that require Body skill are the hardest to get promoted in. Since body- improving activities drain Energy, these Sims end up having less time in the day to maintain motives and make friends.

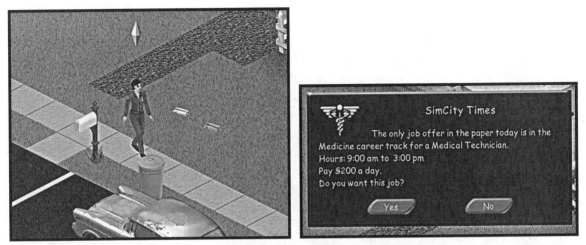

Fig. 6-1. Personality traits can increase the speed with which a Sim acquires corresponding skills. Outgoing types develop Charisma more quickly, for example.

HOW TO GET THE CAREER YOU ALWAYS WANTED

CAREER TRACK	NECESSARY SKILLS	CORRESPONDING PERSONALITY TRAITS
Business	Logic, Charisma	Outgoing
Entertainment	Charisma, Creativity	Outgoing, Playful
Law Enforcement	Logic, Body	Active
Life of Crime	Creativity, Charisma	Playful, Outgoing
Medicine	Logic, Body	Active
Military	Repair, Body	Active
Politics	Charisma, Logic	Outgoing
Pro Athlete	Body, Charisma	Active, Outgoing
Science	Logic, Creativity	Playful
Xtreme	Creativity, Body/Charisma (tie)	Playful, Active, Outgoing

TIP

If the house you build keeps your Sims reasonably happy, you buy a little freedom. An efficient home and objects that satisfy basic Sim needs allow you to leave your game running autonomously without your Sims losing their jobs.

Getting a Job

Sims never seek employment on their own. And if you order Sims to look for a job, they'll comply only if they're in a good mood.

Jobs are plentiful in the Sim world. You'll find one (and only one) position posted in the newspaper every day. But here's a tip: if you desire a different career track from the one you see in the paper, you needn't wait for the next day's paper delivery, even if your funds are very limited. Instead, try the following trick:

Fig. 6-2. Buy a desk, chair, and computer the minute you move a Sim family onto a new lot. A computer allows you to choose from THREE jobs. And, if money's tight, you can sell back the equipment for a full cash refund when you're done!

When you first place your Sim family on a lot, don't buy anything until you check the newspaper for that day's job offer. If it's not the career you want, buy a cheap desk, chair, and computer. Do your job search on the computer, which offers *three* job choices instead of one. Take a job in your desired career track and then sell back the computer, desk, and chair.

If you return the equipment the same day you bought the items, you get a full refund, no depreciation. And, hey, if the three online job choices don't thrill you either, return the equipment anyway and repeat the purchase-return trick the next day.

Job Performance

Mood is the key to job performance, which is updated daily. The game averages every working Sim's current mood with the previous day's performance rating. High mood ratings lead to promotions. Low ratings lead to demotions.

Promotion

Promotions are nice things. The salary boost is usually significant, and most promotions include a generous cash bonus. Each hop up the career ladder requires a specific number of family friends and skills. (Click your Sim's Job button in the Control Panel to view requirements for the next level.) Regardless of mood, if your Sim doesn't meet these criteria, your Sim won't get promoted.

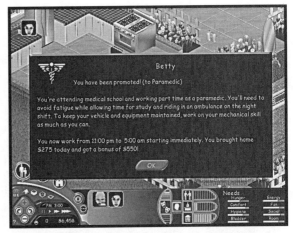

Fig. 6-3. To get promoted, your Sims must build appropriate skills, make friends, and go to work in a good mood.

Fortunately, the first promotion in any career track requires no specific friends or skills. Unless they're miserable, your Sims will find it easy to climb their careers' first rungs.

After a Sim builds enough skill and acquires enough friends to advance to the next job level, the random chance for promotion is skewed by daily job performance. In other words, the better the mood, the better the job performance, and thus the greater the odds for promotion. Thus, sending your Sims to work in a good mood (theirs, not yours) is important.

Do your best to fulfill all your Sims' needs before they go to work each day. Best bet: send your Sims to bed early so they can rise at least two hours before the car pool arrives the next morning. This gives you time to satisfy basic physical needs, such as Hunger, Bladder, and Hygiene (which degrade significantly during a full night's sleep), *before* they head to work.

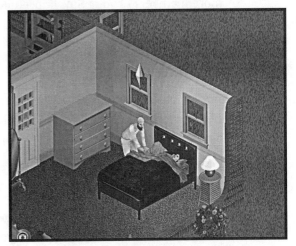

Fig. 6-4. Get your Sims to bed early enough to get a full Energy boost, yet still have time in the morning to satisfy basic physical needs before work.

TIP

Good job performance alone isn't enough to climb the career ladder. Your Sims must hone the skills their jobs require. Check the Job Panel periodically to find out what the skills are and learn how to improve them.

> ## Tips from the Testers
>
> My favorite career track is the Military. It's high-paying in the early levels, so you get a great start, and you don't need to worry about making and maintaining friends until your Sim tries for the Level 6 position, Flight Officer. Entering the Military track is a great way for players new to *The Sims* to start out.
>
> —Andrew Blomquist, Tester

Friend Requirement

Here's a happy fact. The friend requirement for a job promotion refers to "family friends"—that is, friends of your household. So if another Sim in your household has made a friend, that person counts as a family friend for you, too. Fellow household members don't count as family friends for purposes of job promotion, however. If two or more members of your Sim household share the same friend, that friend counts as a family friend only once.

Fig. 6-5. You can't get to the top in any career without plenty of family friends. Have your Sims socialize as much as possible.

Demotion

A poor job performance increases a Sim's risk for demotion. In fact, performance is the *only* factor. Missing work is irrelevant. Losing friends or skill is irrelevant. To prevent demotions, send your Sims to work in a good mood.

Getting Fired

A Sim who misses work two days in a row gets sacked—no excuses, no arbitration, no severance package. Just a phone call—*good-bye*. This is the *only* way to get fired. (Note that you can skip one day of work with no repercussions other than lost wages, unless you have a night job. With night jobs, you lose your job the first time you miss work.)

Unfortunately, getting fired knocks a Sim completely out of the current career track and back to square one. Any new position will be entry level, even if it's in the same career track as the job the Sim squandered.

Tips from the Testers

It's entirely possible for a Sim to go to work only every other day and still succeed. I wouldn't recommend this until your Sim gets a few promotions and a decent salary. But a Sim who reaches about Level 4 should find it relatively easy to get by working only every other day.

Use days off to build skills and make friends. As soon as you can afford skill-building equipment (chessboard, exercise machine, and so on), skip two days of work to get fired, and then focus on skills. Once you have skills, it's pretty easy to advance back up the career ladder. Job promotions are difficult to earn only when your Sim is just starting out and has no skills at all.

—Andrew Blomquist, Tester

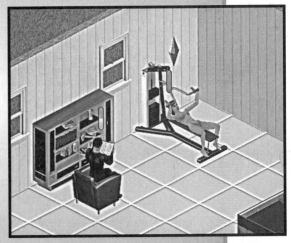

Fig. 6-6. Let your Sims take a day off every few days to focus on building skills and making new friends.

Workday Motive Decay

When Sims are home, their need scores drop at a standard rate, modified somewhat by personality traits and living conditions. This standard motive decay is turned off, however, when the Sims are at work.

Each job affects motives in a different way. For example, Law Enforcement positions suffer far greater on-the-job Comfort decay than other careers (especially Captain Hero with his tight costume), yet somewhat less Hunger decay (all those donut stops, you know). Pro Athletes come home with spent Energy and Hygiene levels. Criminals and Politicians return with lower Social scores. (Coincidence? We think not.) Military personnel suffer the biggest Fun drain. Apparently, getting shot at is kind of a drag.

Refer to the tables in "The 10 Career Tracks" section to learn the daily motive decay rate for each job.

Car Pool

Car pool vehicles arrive one hour before work starts and wait for an hour. (Starting times often differ for each job. Again, see "The 10 Career Tracks" tables.) Sims in a good mood go to work autonomously—that is, they don their work clothes and walk out to the car pool when it arrives. If they're in a bad mood, however, you must direct them to go to work. A worker leaving for the car pool with less than 15 minutes to spare will run to the vehicle.

Tips from the Testers

Although the car pool may arrive at, say, 8 a.m., your Sim needn't *catch* it at 8 a.m. Don't waste an hour by jumping right into the car pool as soon as it arrives. As long as you've started routing your Sim to it by one minute before it leaves, the car pool will wait. Have your Sims build their motives during that hour so they have a successful day at work.

—Andrew Blomquist, Tester

Fig. 6-7. Don't go right to the car pool when it arrives! The car waits one hour, and your Sims can wait until the very last minute—literally. Use the time to boost motive scores or skills.

Chance Cards

Career "chance cards" (dialog boxes describing some event that happened at work) come up periodically after work. These cards add or subtract skill points and/or money. Here's a frightening game fact: hitting Level 10 (the highest level) in any career gives your Sim a 1-in-20 chance of drawing a chance card that switches him or her to a lower level in another career!

Skill Building

Sims don't build skills autonomously. You must direct the little folks to better them-selves. (Of course, Sims in a bad mood won't engage in any skill-building activity except to earn Body points in the pool.) Once a Sim earns a skill point by interacting with a particular skill-building object—say, playing piano for Creativity—the Sim may continue using that object until the mood rating drops below a certain value.

Sims may engage in skill-building activities even after maxing out their skills. For example, a Sim with a Body skill rating of 10 can still work out on an exercise machine. Why you would inflict such punishment on an innocent Sim is between you and your conscience, however.

CAUTION

Repairing appliances without calling a Repairman can be dangerous. Sims with low Mechanical skill can get electrocuted when fixing electronics. Hit the bookshelf and "Study Mechanical." Also, the better a Sim's Mechanical skill, the more quickly the Sim can repair broken objects. Naturally, the Repairman has the best Mechanical skill of all, but he charges §50 per hour.

How to Improve Skills

Each succeeding skill point takes longer and longer to earn. A Sim may need to engage in a skill-building activity for only one hour to get the first skill point. Gaining the second skill point will take two hours, the third three hours, and so on. See Exit Conditions on page 53 for more info.

The game manual lists the objects Sims must use to improve their skills. The following list includes a few notes about each.

SKILL	METHOD OF ENHANCEMENT	NOTES
Cooking	Bookshelf (Study Cooking)	Type of bookshelf (cheap or expensive) has no effect on skill activity.
Mechanical	Bookshelf (Study Mechanical)	Type of bookshelf (cheap or expensive) has no effect on skill activity.
Body	Exercise Machine (Work Out)	Exercise machine increases skill four times faster than the pool. Active Sims acquire skill more quickly.
Body	Pool (Swim)	Pool increases skill four times more slowly than the exercise machine. Active Sims acquire skill more quickly.
Charisma	Mirrors or Medicine Cabinet (Practice Speech)	Outgoing Sims acquire skill more quickly.
Creativity	Easel (Paint)	Playful Sims acquire skill more quickly.
Creativity	Piano (Play)	Playful Sims acquire skill more quickly.
Logic	Chessboard (Play)	Playing with another Sim nets you Social points

Fig. 6-8. A bookshelf, no matter how cheap, lets your Sims bone up on Cooking and Mechanical skills.

Tips from the Testers

Always buy a bookshelf right away. If money is tight, buy the cheapest one. Use bookshelves to raise Cooking skills to lower the risk of cooking fires and increase the value of cooked food. A Sim can study Maintenance skills, as well, to effectively eliminate the need to call the Repairman and fork over $50 per hour every time something breaks.

—Syruss Flyte, Tester

The 10 Career Tracks

The following tables list the salaries, hours, car pool vehicles, and job level requirements for the 10 career tracks. Also listed is the daily decay rate for each motive when the Sim is at work.

NOTE

All children go to school daily from 9 a.m. to 3 p.m. The school bus arrives at 8 a.m. and leaves by 9 a.m.

REQUIREMENTS FOR LEVEL 1 POSITIONS

CAREER TRACK	POSITION	DAILY PAY	HOURS	CAR POOL VEHICLE	COOKING	REPAIR	CHARISMA	BODY	LOGIC	CREATIVITY	FAMILY FRIENDS	DAILY MOTIVE DECAY (HUNGER/COMFORT/ HYGIENE/BLADDER/ ENERGY/FUN/SOCIAL)
Business	Mail Room	§120	9 a.m.–3 p.m.	Junker	0	0	0	0	0	0	0	0/0/0/0/-30/0/0
Entertainment	Waiter/Waitress	§100	9 a.m.–3 p.m.	Junker	0	0	0	0	0	0	0	0/0/0/0/-30/0/0
Law Enforcement	Security Guard	§240	12 a.m.–6 a.m.	Squad Car	0	0	0	0	0	0	0	0/0/0/0/-30/0/0
Life of Crime	Pickpocket	§140	9 a.m.–3 p.m.	Junker	0	0	0	0	0	0	0	0/0/0/0/-/-30/0/0
Medicine	Medical Technician	§200	9 a.m.–3 p.m.	Junker	0	0	0	0	0	0	0	0/0/0/0/-30/0/0
Military	Recruit	§250	6 a.m.–12 p.m.	Military Jeep	0	0	0	0	0	0	0	0/0/-15/0/-30/0/0
Politics	Campaign Work	§220	9 a.m.–6 p.m.	Junker	0	0	0	0	0	0	0	0/0/0/0/-30/0/0
Pro Athlete	Team Mascot	§110	12 p.m.–6 p.m.	Junker	0	0	0	0	0	0	0	0/0/-5/0/-35/0/0
Science	Test Subject	§155	9 a.m.–3 p.m.	Junker	0	0	0	0	0	0	0	0/0/0/0/-30/0/0
Xtreme	Daredevil	§175	9 a.m.–3 p.m.	Junker	0	0	0	0	0	0	0	0/0/0/0/-30/0/0

REQUIREMENTS FOR LEVEL 2 POSITIONS

CAREER TRACK	POSITION	DAILY PAY	HOURS	CAR POOL VEHICLE	COOKING	REPAIR	CHARISMA	BODY	LOGIC	CREATIVITY	FAMILY FRIENDS	DAILY MOTIVE DECAY (HUNGER/COMFORT/ HYGIENE/BLADDER/ ENERGY/FUN/SOCIAL)
Business	Executive Assistant	§180	9 a.m.–4 p.m.	Junker	0	0	0	0	0	0	0	0/0/0/0/-34/-2/0
Entertainment	Extra	§150	9 a.m.–3 p.m.	Junker	0	0	0	0	0	0	0	0/0/0/0/-34/-2/0
Law Enforcement	Cadet	§320	9 a.m.–3 p.m.	Squad Car	0	0	0	0	0	0	0	0/0/0/0/-34/-2/0
Life of Crime	Bagman	§200	11 p.m.–7a.m.	Junker	0	0	0	0	0	0	0	0/0/0/0/-34/-2/0
Medicine	Paramedic	§275	11 p.m.–5a.m.	Junker	0	0	0	0	0	0	0	0/0/0/0/-34/-2/0
Military	Elite Forces	§325	7 a.m.–1 p.m.	Military Jeep	0	0	0	0	0	0	0	0/0/-15/0/-34/-2/0
Politics	Intern	§300	9 a.m.–3 p.m.	Junker	0	0	0	0	0	0	0	0/0/0/0/-34/-2/0
Pro Athlete	Minor Leaguer	§170	9 a.m.–3 p.m.	Junker	0	0	0	0	0	0	0	0/0/-10/0/-40/-2/0
Science	Lab Assistant	§230	11 p.m.–5a.m.	Junker	0	0	0	0	0	0	0	0/0/0/0/-34/-2/0
Xtreme	Bungee Jump Instructor	§250	9 a.m.–3 p.m.	Junker	0	0	0	0	0	0	0	0/0/0/0/-34/-2/0

REQUIREMENTS FOR LEVEL 3 POSITIONS

CAREER TRACK	POSITION	DAILY PAY	HOURS	CAR POOL VEHICLE	COOKING	REPAIR	CHARISMA	BODY	LOGIC	CREATIVITY	FAMILY FRIENDS	DAILY MOTIVE DECAY (HUNGER/COMFORT/ HYGIENE/BLADDER/ ENERGY/FUN/SOCIAL)
Business	Field Sales Rep	§250	9 a.m.–4 p.m.	Junker	0	2	0	0	0	0	0	-3/0/-5/0/-38/-4/0
Entertainment	Bit Player	§200	9 a.m.–3 p.m.	Junker	0	0	2	0	0	0	0	-3/0/-5/0/-38/-4/0
Law Enforcement	Patrol Officer	§380	5 p.m.–1a.m.	Squad Car	0	0	0	2	0	0	0	-3/0/-5/0/-38/-4/0
Life of Crime	Bookie	§275	12 p.m.–7 p.m.	Standard Car	0	0	0	2	0	0	0	-3/0/-5/0/-38/-4/0
Medicine	Nurse	§340	9 a.m.–3 p.m.	Standard Car	0	2	0	0	0	0	0	-3/0/-5/0/-38/-4/0
Military	Drill Instructor	§250	8 a.m.–2 p.m.	Military Jeep	0	0	0	2	0	0	0	-3/0/-20/0/-38/-4/0
Politics	Lobbyist	§360	9 a.m.–3 p.m.	Standard Car	0	0	2	0	0	0	0	-3/0/-5/0/-38/-4/0
Pro Athlete	Rookie	§230	9 a.m.–3 p.m.	Junker	0	0	0	2	0	0	0	-3/0/-15/0/-45/-2/0
Science	Field Researcher	§320	9 a.m.–3 p.m.	Standard Car	0	0	0	0	2	0	0	-3/0/-5/0/-38/-4/0
Xtreme	Whitewater Guide	§325	9 a.m.–3 p.m.	SUV	0	0	0	2	0	0	1	-3/0/-10/0/-45/-4/0

REQUIREMENTS FOR LEVEL 4 POSITIONS

CAREER TRACK	POSITION	DAILY PAY	HOURS	CAR POOL VEHICLE	COOKING	REPAIR	CHARISMA	BODY	LOGIC	CREATIVITY	FAMILY FRIENDS	DAILY MOTIVE DECAY (HUNGER/COMFORT/ HYGIENE/BLADDER/ ENERGY/FUN/SOCIAL)
Business	Junior Executive	§320	9 a.m.–4 p.m.	Standard Car	0	2	2	0	0	0	1	-7/0/-10/0/-42/-7/0
Entertainment	Stunt Double	§275	9 a.m.–4 p.m.	Standard Car	0	0	2	2	0	0	2	-7/0/-10/0/-42/-7/00
Law Enforcement	Desk Sergeant	§440	9 a.m.–3 p.m.	Squad Car	0	2	0	2	0	0	1	-7/0/-10/0/-42/-7/0
Life of Crime	Con Artist	§350	9 a.m.–3 p.m.	Standard Car	0	0	1	2	0	1	2	-7/0/-10/0/-42/-7/0
Medicine	Intern	§410	9 a.m.–6 p.m.	Standard Car	0	2	0	2	0	0	2	-7/0/-10/0/-42/-7/0
Military	Junior Officer	§450	9 a.m.–3 p.m.	Military Jeep	0	1	2	2	0	0	0	-7/0/-20/0/-42/-8/0
Politics	Campaign Manager	§430	9 a.m.–6 p.m.	Standard Car	0	0	2	0	1	0	2	-7/0/-10/0/-42/-7/0
Pro Athlete	Starter	§300	9 a.m.–3 p.m.	Standard Car	0	0	0	5	0	0	1	-7/0/-20/0/-50/-2/0
Science	Science Teacher	§375	9 a.m.–4 p.m.	Standard Car	0	0	1	0	3	0	1	-7/0/-10/0/-40/-7/0
Xtreme	Xtreme Circuit Pro	§400	9 a.m.–3 p.m.	SUV	0	1	0	4	0	0	2	-7/0/-20/0/-50/-2/0

REQUIREMENTS FOR LEVEL 5 POSITIONS

CAREER TRACK	POSITION	DAILY PAY	HOURS	CAR POOL VEHICLE	COOKING	REPAIR	CHARISMA	BODY	LOGIC	CREATIVITY	FAMILY FRIENDS	DAILY MOTIVE DECAY (HUNGER/COMFORT/ HYGIENE/BLADDER/ ENERGY/FUN/SOCIAL)
Business	Executive	§400	9 a.m.–4 p.m.	Standard Car	0	2	2	0	2	0	3	-10/0/-15/0/-46/-10/0
Entertainment	B-Movie Star	§375	10 a.m.–5 p.m.	Standard Car	0	0	3	3	0	1	4	-10/0/-15/0/-46/-10/0
Law Enforcement	Vice Squad	§490	10 p.m.–4a.m.	Squad Car	0	3	0	4	0	0	2	-10/0/-15/0/-46/-10/0
Life of Crime	Getaway Driver	§425	5 p.m.–1a.m.	Standard Car	0	2	1	2	0	2	3	-10/0/-10/0/-46/-10/0
Medicine	Resident	§480	9 p.m.–4a.m.	Standard Car	0	3	0	2	2	0	3	-10/0/-15/0/-46/-10/0
Military	Counter-Intelligence	§500	9 a.m.–3 p.m.	Military Jeep	1	1	2	4	0	0	0	-10/0/-25/0/-46/-12/0
Politics	City Council Member	§485	9 a.m.–3 p.m.	Town Car	0	0	3	1	1	0	4	-10/0/-15/0/-46/-8/0
Pro Athlete	All-Star	§385	9 a.m.–3 p.m.	SUV	0	1	1	6	0	0	3	-10/0/-25/0/-55/-3/0
Science	Project Leader	§450	9 a.m.–5 p.m.	Standard Car	0	0	2	0	4	1	3	-10/0/-12/0/-43/-8/0
Xtreme	Bush Pilot	§475	9 a.m.–3 p.m.	SUV	1	2	0	4	1	0	3	-10/0/-15/0/-46/-5/-10

REQUIREMENTS FOR LEVEL 6 POSITIONS

CAREER TRACK	POSITION	DAILY PAY	HOURS	CAR POOL VEHICLE	COOKING	REPAIR	CHARISMA	BODY	LOGIC	CREATIVITY	FAMILY FRIENDS	DAILY MOTIVE DECAY (HUNGER/COMFORT/ HYGIENE/BLADDER/ ENERGY/FUN/SOCIAL)
Business	Senior Manager	§520	9 a.m.–4 p.m.	Standard Car	0	2	3	0	3	2	6	-14/0/-20/0/-50/-13/0
Entertainment	Supporting Player	§500	10 a.m.–6 p.m.	Limo	0	1	4	4	0	2	6	-14/0/-20/0/-50/-13/0
Law Enforcement	Detective	§540	9 a.m.–3 p.m.	Squad Car	1	3	1	5	1	0	4	-14/0/-20/0/-50/-13/0
Life of Crime	Bank Robber	§530	3 p.m.–11 p.m.	Town Car	0	3	2	3	1	2	4	-14/0/-15/0/-50/-13/-5
Medicine	GP	§550	10 a.m.–6 p.m.	Town Car	0	3	1	3	4	0	4	-14/0/-20/0/-50/-13/0
Military	Flight Officer	§550	9 a.m.–3 p.m.	Military Jeep	1	2	4	4	1	0	1	-14/0/-28/0/-50/-15/0
Politics	State Assembly-person	§540	9 a.m.–4 p.m.	Town Car	0	0	4	2	1	1	6	-14/0/-20/0/-50/-12/-3
Pro Athlete	MVP	§510	9 a.m.–3 p.m.	SUV	0	2	2	7	0	0	5	-14/0/-30/0/-60/-4/0
Science	Inventor	§540	10 a.m.–7 p.m.	Town Car	0	2	2	0	4	3	4	-14/0/-15/0/-45/-9/-8
Xtreme	Mountain Climber	§550	9 a.m.–3 p.m.	SUV	1	4	0	6	1	0	4	-14/0/-30/0/-60/0/0

REQUIREMENTS FOR LEVEL 7 POSITIONS

Career Track	Position	Daily Pay	Hours	Car Pool Vehicle	Cooking	Repair	Charisma	Body	Logic	Creativity	Family Friends	Daily Motive Decay (Hunger/Comfort/ Hygiene/Bladder/ Energy/Fun/Social)
Business	Vice President	§660	9 a.m.–5 p.m.	Town Car	0	2	4	2	4	2	8	-18/0/-25/0/-54/-16/0
Entertainment	TV Star	§650	10 a.m.–6 p.m.	Limo	0	1	6	5	0	3	8	-18/0/-25/0/-54/-16/0
Law Enforcement	Lieutenant	§590	9 a.m.–3 p.m.	Limo	1	3	2	5	3	1	6	-18/0/-25/0/-54/-16/0
Life of Crime	Cat Burglar	§640	9 p.m.–3a.m.	Town Car	1	3	2	5	2	3	6	-18/0/-20/0/-54/-16/0
Medicine	Specialist	§625	10 p.m.–4a.m.	Town Car	0	4	2	4	4	1	5	-18/0/-25/0/-54/-16/0
Military	Senior Officer	§580	9 a.m.–3 p.m.	Military Jeep	1	3	4	5	3	0	3	-18/0/-31/0/-55/-20/0
Politics	Congressperson	§600	9 a.m.–3 p.m.	Town Car	0	0	4	3	3	2	9	-18/0/-25/0/-54/-18/-7
Pro Athlete	Superstar	§680	9 a.m.–4 p.m.	SUV	1	2	3	8	0	0	7	-18/0/-35/0/-65/-5/0
Science	Scholar	§640	10 a.m.–3 p.m.	Town Car	0	4	2	0	6	4	5	-18/0/-20/0/-48/-10/-10
Xtreme	Photojournalist	§650	9 a.m.–3 p.m.	SUV	1	5	2	6	1	3	5	-18/0/-25/0/-54/-16/0

REQUIREMENTS FOR LEVEL 8 POSITIONS

Career Track	Position	Daily Pay	Hours	Car Pool Vehicle	Cooking	Repair	Charisma	Body	Logic	Creativity	Family Friends	Daily Motive Decay (Hunger/Comfort/ Hygiene/Bladder/ Energy/Fun/Social)
Business	President	§800	9 a.m.–5 p.m.	Town Car	0	2	5	2	6	3	10	-22/0/-30/0/-58/-19/0
Entertainment	Feature Star	§900	5 p.m.–1a.m.	Limo	0	2	7	6	0	4	10	-22/0/-30/0/-58/-19/0
Law Enforcement	SWAT Team Leader	§625	9 a.m.–3 p.m.	Limo	1	4	3	6	5	1	8	-22/0/-30/0/-58/-19/0
Life of Crime	Counterfeiter	§760	9 p.m.–3a.m.	Town Car	1	5	2	5	3	5	8	-22/0/-25/0/-58/-19/-15
Medicine	Surgeon	§700	10 p.m.–4a.m.	Town Car	0	4	3	5	6	2	7	-22/0/-30/0/-58/-19/0
Military	Commander	§600	9 a.m.–3 p.m.	Military Jeep	1	6	5	5	5	0	5	-22/0/-33/0/-60/-25/0
Politics	Judge	§650	9 a.m.–3 p.m.	Town Car	0	0	5	4	4	3	11	-22/0/-30/0/-58/-22/-11
Pro Athlete	Assistant Coach	§850	9 a.m.–2 p.m.	SUV	2	2	4	9	0	1	9	-22/0/-40/0/-70/-6/0
Science	Top Secret Researcher	§740	10 a.m.–3 p.m.	Town Car	1	6	4	0	7	4	7	-22/0/-25/0/-52/-12/-13
Xtreme	Treasure Hunter	§725	10 a.m.–5 p.m.	SUV	1	6	3	7	3	4	7	-22/0/-34/0/-60/-15/-5

REQUIREMENTS FOR LEVEL 9 POSITIONS

CAREER TRACK	POSITION	DAILY PAY	HOURS	CAR POOL VEHICLE	COOKING	REPAIR	CHARISMA	BODY	LOGIC	CREATIVITY	FAMILY FRIENDS	DAILY MOTIVE DECAY (HUNGER/COMFORT/HYGIENE/BLADDER/ENERGY/FUN/SOCIAL)
Business	CEO	§950	9 a.m.–4 p.m.	Limo	0	2	6	2	7	5	12	-26/0/-35/0/-62/-22/0
Entertainment	Broadway Star	§1100	10 a.m.–5 p.m.	Limo	0	2	8	7	0	7	12	-26/0/-35/0/-62/-22/0
Law Enforcement	Police Chief	§650	9 a.m.–5 p.m.	Limo	1	4	4	7	7	3	10	-26/0/-35/0/-62/-22/0
Life of Crime	Smuggler	§900	9 a.m.–3 p.m.	Town Car	1	5	5	6	3	6	10	-26/0/-30/0/-62/-22/-20
Medicine	Medical Researcher	§775	9 p.m.–4a.m.	Limo	0	5	4	6	8	3	9	-26/0/-35/0/-62/-22/0
Military	Astronaut	§625	9 a.m.–3 p.m.	Limo	1	9	5	8	6	0	6	-26/0/-35/0/-65/-30/0
Politics	Senator	§700	9 a.m.–6 p.m.	Limo	0	0	6	5	6	4	14	-26/0/-35/0/-62/-26/-15
Pro Athlete	Coach	§1000	9 a.m.–3 p.m.	SUV	3	2	6	10	0	2	11	-26/0/-45/0/-75/-8/0
Science	Theorist	§870	10 a.m.–2 p.m.	Town Car	1	7	4	0	9	7	8	-26/0/-30/0/-56/-16/-16
Xtreme	Grand Prix Driver	§825	10 a.m.–4 p.m.	Bentley	1	6	5	7	5	7	9	-26/0/-35/0/-62/-5/-10

REQUIREMENTS FOR LEVEL 10 POSITIONS

CAREER TRACK	POSITION	DAILY PAY	HOURS	CAR POOL VEHICLE	COOKING	REPAIR	CHARISMA	BODY	LOGIC	CREATIVITY	FAMILY FRIENDS	DAILY MOTIVE DECAY (HUNGER/COMFORT/HYGIENE/BLADDER/ENERGY/FUN/SOCIAL)
Business	Business Tycoon	§1200	9 a.m.–3 p.m.	Limo	0	2	8	2	9	6	14	-30/0/-40/0/-66/-25/0
Entertainment	Superstar	§1400	10 a.m.–3 p.m.	Limo	0	2	10	8	0	10	14	-30/0/-40/0/-66/-25/0
Law Enforcement	Captain Hero	§700	10 a.m.–4 p.m.	Limo	1	4	6	7	10	5	12	-20/-80/-45/-25/-60/0/0
Life of Crime	Criminal Mastermind	§1100	6 p.m.–12a.m.	Limo	2	5	7	6	4	8	12	-30/0/-35/0/-66/-25/-25
Medicine	Chief of Hospital Staff	§850	9 p.m.–4a.m.	Limo	0	6	6	7	9	4	11	-30/0/-40/0/-66/-25/0
Military	General	§650	9 a.m.–3 p.m.	Staff Sedan	1	10	7	10	9	0	8	-30/0/-40/0/-70/-35/0
Politics	Mayor	§750	9 a.m.–3 p.m.	Limo	0	0	9	5	7	5	17	-30/0/-40/0/-66/-30/-20
Pro Athlete	Hall of Famer	§1300	9 a.m.–3 p.m.	Limo	4	2	9	10	0	3	13	-30/0/-50/0/-80/-10/0
Science	Mad Scientist	§1000	10 a.m.–2 p.m.	Limo	2	8	5	0	10	10	10	-30/0/-35/0/-60/-20/-20
Xtreme	International Spy	§925	11 a.m.–5 p.m.	Bentley	2	6	8	8	6	9	11	-30/0/-30/0/-70/-20/-15

School

Sim kids don't have careers, of course. But they do have to go to school and keep their grades up. Slackers face expulsion from the family (and the game) by being sent to Military School. Here's the lowdown on academics in *The Sims*.

Going to School

The school bus arrives daily at 8 a.m. outside households that include Sim kids. Kids with mood ratings in the

Fig. 6-9. Send your kids to the school bus in a good mood to boost Report Card grades each day.

green go to the bus automatically unless you direct them to another activity. A Sim kid who goes to a bus that's been waiting more than 45 minutes runs to it automatically.

The Report Card

Click on the Job button on the Control Panel to view your Sim kid's current Report Card, which displays a single grade. This grade improves a level—from B+ to A-, for example—every day the kid rides the bus to school in a good mood. Of course, the reverse is true,

Fig. 6-10. Keep an eye on that Report Card grade. If it drops to a D or below, try boosting it with some home study.

as well. The Report Card grade drops a level every day the kid leaves in a bad mood.

Kids who maintain an A+ Report Card randomly get small cash awards, accompanied by dialog such as, "Beth just won the spelling bee at school. Grandma sends her §100."

Studying for School

Each kid starts out with a B grade. Children with grades lower than A+ are given the pie-menu choice to Study for School when you click on a bookshelf. Kids don't *have* to study at home if they continue to attend school in a good mood. But it's one way to speed up grade inflation.

Kids with poor grades needn't study as long as higher-grade students to raise their grades. An F student need study only 20 minutes to get to a D-, 30 minutes to go from D- to D, 40 minutes from D to D+, and so on. This way, you can home-school your kids if you want, but doing so requires far more effort than if they rode the bus daily to school.

Of course, Sim kids won't study autonomously; you must direct them to. (*The Sims* is based on real life, after all.) Worse, kids won't study if they're in a bad mood. Overall, unhappy kids are unsuccessful kids.

Playing Hooky and Military School

Sim kids go to school autonomously in the morning if they're in a good mood. If they don't, you must encourage them to catch the morning bus. Every day a kid cuts classes, that kid's Report Card drops an entire letter grade—for example, from B- to C-. When the grade drops to D or below, a dialog box threatens your kid with Military School.

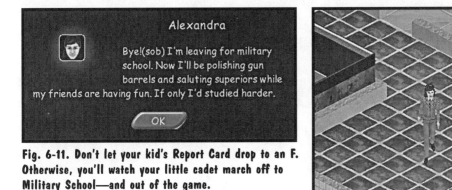

Fig. 6-11. Don't let your kid's Report Card drop to an F. Otherwise, you'll watch your little cadet march off to Military School—and out of the game.

If the Report Card is already at D or below when the bus arrives in the morning, you'll hear warning music and view a flashing Report Card. Last chance! Finally, if the grade drops to F, it's off to Military School with the little delinquent, who leaves the family forever—and nails your household with a $1,000 one-time charge for tuition. Ouch!

7
Sim Economics
101

Today's lecture covers the inexorable flow of simoleans, goods, services, and other sundry elements that make up *The Sims'* economic system. In particular, we explore how Sim objects depreciate (and, in some cases, appreciate) in worth, and explain how the SimCity Savings & Loan calculates those pesky bills you get in the mail every three days.

Fig. 7-1. The Holy Simolean. End-all, be-all? Or just another grand illusion? Fortunately, there's no room for philosophical musing in a strategy guide.

After that, we discuss the various services available to your Sim household. Finally, let us together stroll some of the darker side streets of Sim life—fire, theft, accident—and learn how to avoid or minimize losses from such disasters.

TIP

The hardest part of *The Sims* is starting a fresh family and advancing its members. Once you've established Family A (we'll call them the Waltons) with good jobs and a solid net worth, consider marrying or moving high-income members into a Family B (the Newbies) that's just starting out.

The Walton member's high wages can help stabilize the Newbies quickly, freeing up Newbie members to build skills and make friends for their own advancement. It may seem kind of mercenary, but you can always marry the Walton member back into his or her original family later.

NOTE
Check out "Cheats & Quick Start Tips" to learn ways (some delightfully underhanded) to build money quickly in the early phases of your neighborhood.

Net Worth

With the exception of the Goths and the Newbies, all families start with a net worth of 20,000 simoleans. Net worth includes lot price, the depreciated value of the house (and other architectural items), the depreciated value of objects, and household funds. Lots come in three sizes; size and location determine

Fig. 7-2. Every new family starts with 20,000 simoleans. The bigger the family, the more money you should allocate to house size and multiple bathrooms. (Crowded bathrooms block the flow of happiness in ANY home.)

lot cost. When a family moves, all purchased objects are deleted from the house and the depreciated value is credited to the family's funds.

Object Depreciation

Object depreciation is relevant to your Sim family's net worth and bill amounts, and to the amount of money you get when you sell objects. Each object you purchase (other than art objects, which follow different rules) has an initial and daily depreciation, as well as a depreciation limit.

Initial Depreciation

You may return the stuff you buy for a full refund before midnight on the day of your purchase. After your Sims own an item for one full Sim day, however, its worth decreases by an initial depreciation value—a percentage of the object's original cost. This percentage varies according to the object's category when sorted by function in the catalog—Electronics, Decorative, Lighting, and so forth.

The Object Depreciation table at the end of this section provides a complete list of items and their initial depreciation.

Daily Depreciation

Again, the initial depreciation lowers an item's value after midnight on the day of purchase. After that, the item continues to depreciate at a fixed amount every Sim day until it reaches a limit. (See the following "Depreciation Limit" section.) This daily depreciation is 1 percent of the item's original value.

The Object Depreciation table later in this section provides a complete list of items and their daily depreciation.

Depreciation Limit

Every item's value decreases by an initial depreciation after midnight on the day of purchase, and then drops daily to a given limit. Once it reaches this value, it remains there for the rest of its stay in your household. The Object Depreciation table provides a complete list of items and their depreciation limits.

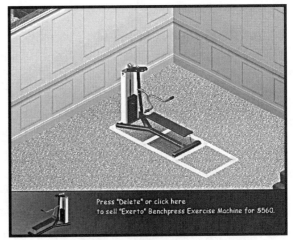

Press "Delete" or click here
to sell "Exerto" Benchpress Exercise Machine for §560.

Fig. 7-3. Most items you can purchase in THE SIMS depreciate. This Exerto exercise machine originally cost §700, but it's depreciated §140 over time.

Value of Broken Items

Oops! I dropped it. Too bad. If you sell a broken object, you get only half its current depreciated value. Hey, what did you expect?

Art Appreciation/Depreciation

Paintings and sculptures appreciate and depreciate randomly every day. In general, the trend is upward. Beyond that, all we can say is it's up to the whims of the snooty Sim art crowd.

OBJECT DEPRECIATION

PURCHASE PRICE	NAME	INITIAL DEPRECIATION	DAILY DEPRECIATION	DEPRECIATION LIMIT
§50	Alarm: Smoke	§12	§0	§10
§250	Alarm: Burglar	§62	§2	§50
§200	Aquarium	§30	§2	§80
§800	Bar	§120	§8	§320
§350	Barbecue	§70	§4	§105
§650	Basketball Hoop	§98	§6	§260

OBJECT DEPRECIATION, continued

PURCHASE PRICE	NAME	INITIAL DEPRECIATION	DAILY DEPRECIATION	DEPRECIATION LIMIT
§450	Bed: Double (Cheap Eaze)	§68	§4	§180
§1,000	Bed: Double (Napolean)	§150	§10	§400
§3,000	Bed: Double (Mission)	§450	§30	§1,200
§300	Bed: Single (Spartan)	§45	§3	§120
§450	Bed: Single (Tyke Nyte)	§68	§4	§180
§250	Bench: Garden	§38	§2	§100
§250	Bookshelf: Pine	§38	§2	§100
§500	Bookshelf: Amishim	§75	§5	§200
§900	Bookshelf: Libri di Regina	§135	§9	§360
§150	Chair: Deck	§22	§2	§60
§80	Chair: Dining (Werkbunnst)	§12	§1	§32
§200	Chair: Dining (Teak)	§30	§2	§80
§600	Chair: Dining (Empress)	§90	§6	§240
§1,200	Chair: Dining (Parisienne)	§180	§12	§480
§80	Chair: Living Room (Wicker)	§12	§1	§32
§250	Chair: Living Room (Country Class)	§38	§2	§100
§450	Chair: Living Room (Citronel)	§68	§4	§180
§500	Chair: Living Room (Sarrbach)	§75	§5	§200
§100	Chair: Office	§15	§1	§40
§250	Chair: Recliner (Back Slack)	§38	§2	§100
§850	Chair: Recliner (Von Braun)	§128	§8	§340
§500	Chess Set	§75	§5	§200
§30	Clock: Alarm	§4	§0	§12
§3,500	Clock: Grandfather	§525	§35	§1,400
§450	Coffee: Espresso Machine	§90	§4	§135
§85	Coffeemaker	§17	§1	§26
§999	Computer (Moneywell)	§250	§10	§200
§1,800	Computer (Microscotch)	§450	§18	§360
§2,800	Computer (Brahma 2000)	§700	§28	§560
§6,500	Computer (Marco)	§1,625	§65	§1,300
§400	Counter: Bath (Count Blanc)	§60	§4	§160
§150	Counter: Kitchen (NuMica)	§22	§2	§60

Purchase Price	Name	Initial Depreciation	Daily Depreciation	Depreciation Limit
§250	Counter: Kitchen (Tiled)	§38	§2	§100
§800	Counter: Kitchen (Barcelona: Out)	§120	§8	§320
§800	Counter: Kitchen (Barcelona: In)	§120	§8	§320
§80	Desk (Mesquite)	§12	§1	§32
§220	Desk (Cupertino)	§33	§2	§88
§800	Desk (Redmond)	§120	§8	§320
§550	Dishwasher (Dish Duster)	§110	§6	§165
§950	Dishwasher (Fuzzy Logic)	§190	§10	§285
§180	Dollhouse	§27	§2	§72
§250	Dresser (Pinegulcher)	§38	§2	§100
§300	Dresser (Kinderstuff)	§45	§3	§120
§550	Dresser (Oak Armoire)	§82	§6	§220
§1,200	Dresser (Antique Armoire)	§180	§12	§480
§250	Easel	§38	§2	§100
§700	Exercise Machine	§105	§7	§280
§12	Flamingo	§2	§0	§5
§220	Food Processor	§44	§2	§66
§700	Fountain	§105	§7	§280
§600	Fridge (Llamark)	§120	§6	§180
§1,200	Fridge (Porcina)	§240	§12	§360
§2,500	Fridge (Freeze Secret)	§500	§25	§750
§6,500	Hot Tub	§1,300	§65	§1,950
§50	Lamp: Floor (Halogen)	§8	§0	§20
§100	Lamp: Floor (Lumpen)	§15	§1	§40
§350	Lamp: Floor (Torchosteronne)	§52	§4	§140
§50	Lamp: Garden	§7	§1	§20
§25	Lamp: Table (Bottle)	§4	§0	§10
§85	Lamp: Table (Ceramiche)	§13	§1	§34
§180	Lamp: Table (Elite)	§27	§2	§72
§300	Lamp: Table (Antique)	§45	§3	§120
§80	Lamp: Lava	§12	§1	§32
§125	Medicine Cabinet	§19	§1	§50
§250	Microwave	§50	§2	§75
§150	Mirror: Floor	§22	§2	§60

OBJECT DEPRECIATION, continued

PURCHASE PRICE	NAME	INITIAL DEPRECIATION	DAILY DEPRECIATION	DEPRECIATION LIMIT
§100	Mirror: Wall	§15	§1	§40
§50	Phone: Tabletop	§12	§0	§10
§75	Phone: Wall	§19	§1	§15
§3,500	Piano	§525	§35	§1,400
§1,800	Pinball Machine	§450	§18	§360
§120	Plant: Big (Rubber)	§18	§1	§48
§150	Plant: Big (Cactus)	§22	§2	§60
§160	Plant: Big (Jade)	§24	§2	§64
§30	Plant: Small (Violets)	§4	§0	§12
§35	Plant: Small (Spider)	§5	§0	§14
§45	Plant: Small (Geranium)	§7	§0	§18
§1,200	Play Structure	§180	§12	§480
§4,200	Pool Table	§630	§42	§1,680
§650	Shower	§130	§6	§195
§400	Sink: Bathroom Pedestal	§80	§4	§120
§250	Sink: Kitchen (Single)	§50	§2	§75
§500	Sink: Kitchen (Double)	§100	§5	§150
§150	Sofa: Loveseat (Contempo)	§22	§2	§60
§160	Sofa: Loveseat (Indoor-Outdoor)	§24	§2	§64
§340	Sofa: Loveseat (Country)	§51	§3	§136
§360	Sofa: Loveseat (Blue Pinstripe)	§54	§4	§144
§875	Sofa: Loveseat (Luxuriare)	§131	§9	§350
§180	Sofa (Recycled)	§27	§2	§72
§200	Sofa (Contempo)	§30	§2	§80
§220	Sofa (SimSafari)	§33	§2	§88
§400	Sofa (Blue Pinstripe)	§60	§4	§160
§450	Sofa (Country)	§68	§4	§180
§1,100	Sofa (Deiter)	§165	§11	§440
§1,450	Sofa (Dolce)	§218	§14	§580
§100	Stereo: Boom Box	§25	§1	§20
§650	Stereo (Zimantz)	§162	§6	§130

Purchase Price	Name	Initial Depreciation	Daily Depreciation	Depreciation Limit
§2,550	Stereo (Strings)	§638	§26	§510
§400	Stove (Dialectric)	§80	§4	§120
§1,000	Stove (Pyrotorre)	§200	§10	§300
§95	Table: Dining (NuMica)	§14	§1	§38
§200	Table: Dining (Colonial)	§30	§2	§80
§450	Table: Dining (Mesa)	§68	§4	§180
§1,200	Table: Dining (Parisienne)	§180	§12	§480
§40	Table: End (Pinegulcher)	§6	§0	§16
§55	Table: End (Wicker)	§8	§1	§22
§75	Table: End (KinderStuff)	§11	§1	§30
§120	Table: End (Anywhere)	§18	§1	§48
§135	Table: End (Imperious)	§20	§1	§54
§250	Table: End (Mission)	§38	§2	§100
§300	Table: End (Sumpto)	§45	§3	§120
§200	Table: Outdoor (Backwoods)	§30	§2	§80
§100	Toaster Oven	§20	§1	§30
§300	Toilet (Hygeia-O-Matic)	§60	§3	§90
§1,200	Toilet (Flush Force)	§240	§12	§360
§5	Tombstone/Urn	§1	§0	§2
§50	Toy Box	§8	§0	§20
§80	Train Set: Small	§20	§1	§16
§955	Train Set: Large	§239	§10	§191
§375	Trash Compactor	§75	§4	§112
§800	Tub (Justa)	§160	§8	§240
§1,500	Tub (Sani-Queen)	§300	§15	§450
§3,200	Tub (Hydrothera)	§640	§32	§960
§85	TV (Monochrome)	§21	§1	§17
§500	TV (Trottco)	§125	§5	§100
§3,500	TV (Soma)	§875	§35	§700
§2,300	VR Glasses	§575	§23	§460

A Note About Clothes

In *The Sims,* all clothes are free—normal clothes, work clothes, formal wear, swimwear, PJs. Isn't that nice? Not only that, but you can change your Sim's daily outfit at no charge. Well, not exactly *no* charge; you need a dresser or armoire. If you have one, click on it and select Change Clothes. Your Sim will don a different outfit from the one you assigned originally back in the Create a Sim screen. Selecting Change Clothes creates a new default outfit. That is, whenever your Sim takes a shower or bath or gets out of bed, he or she puts on this new set of clothes. Your Sim can also change their body type at the dresser/armoire—losing or gaining 100 pounds!

Build Depreciation

During any Build mode session, you can undo any action you've taken during that session for a full refund. Key words—*during that session!* Click the Undo button to undo the previous action and get a full refund. Click again to undo the *previous* previous action (going back in time), and get another full refund. You can click Undo as many times as you want to undo actions back to the beginning of the current session.

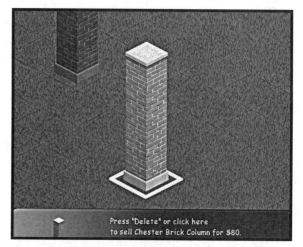

Fig. 7-4. Using the Undo button is the only way to get a full refund when taking back Build mode moves. If you delete or sell back (instead of Undo) this Chester Brick Column, for example, you lose 20 percent of the §100 you paid originally.

Once you leave Build mode, however, you can't return later and undo actions. You can sell most architecture items from previous Build mode sessions, but only for a depreciated value that remains constant no matter how old the item grows.

Also note that in Build mode, using the Undo button is the *only* way to get a full refund. Any other means of deletion, even during the current session, results in the set depreciation. For example, if you place a Chester Brick Column on your lot for §100, and then change your mind, the only way to get a full refund is to click Undo. If you use the Hand Tool to sell the Chester Brick Column or delete it, you'll receive only the column's depreciated value.

Build Items that Depreciate

You can undo the following Build items/actions for a full refund during the current Build mode session. After that, you may sell (or delete) them at a 20 percent depreciation rate (that is, you get back 80 percent of the original purchase price).

Important: Remember that covering over old wall or floor tiles eliminates any refund for them. You must remove (sell or delete) the old wall/floor coverings first in order to get money back.

- Walls
- Wallpaper (if deleted, but not if wallpapered over)
- Floor covering (if deleted, but not if covered over)
- Windows
- Doors
- Pool tiles, ladder, diving board
- Fireplaces
- Stairs

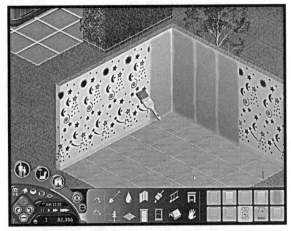

Fig. 7-5. Remember to delete old wall or floor coverings before you place new ones. If you just paper over old wallpaper, you recover NONE of the cost of the original materials.

Build Items You Can't Sell

You may undo the following build items/actions for a full refund during the current Build mode session, but you may not sell them at any time. If you delete them (select them with the Hand Tool and press Delete), you receive no money for them.

- Trees
- Shrubs
- Flowers
- Terrain changes

Bills and the Repo Man

Bills. We all have them. Rich or poor, you can't ignore bills—not in real life, and not in *The Sims*. So don't forget to check the mailbox. The letter carrier delivers bills to your Sims' home every three days. (The red mailbox flag goes up to alert you when bills arrive.) It takes 10 days for bills to become overdue. They turn yellow after three days, orange after six, and red after nine. Pay your bills by the 10th day, or the pitiless Repo Man will pay you a visit.

Bill Calculation

In general, the more items you own, the more you owe. To determine what you owe, the happy accountants at SimCity Savings & Loan calculate 3 percent of the depreciated value of all your billable objects.

NOTE
The mailbox interaction Get Mail advertises with a high attenuation drop-off. That is, Sims must be near the mailbox to "hear" its ad and pick up their mail on their own. So workers returning in car pool at end of the day are likely to get their mail, but those watching TV in the house won't hear the mailbox calling to them.

And what are billable objects? You would ask that question. Billable objects are everything you purchased (including Build mode materials) except columns, doors, paintings, dead plants, sculptures, shrubs, staircases, trees, and windows. Other rather obvious examples of nonbillable objects are ash and trash piles, babies, bills, fires, floods, food, the mailbox, newspapers, and the outdoor trash can. Note that your bills are 10 percent less for each kid in the family, thanks to the dependent tax credit.

Repossession

Fig. 7-6. The Repo Man. You don't want to see this guy. Here he is, sucking up your very bed. Pay your bills within 10 days of receipt to avoid his costly visits.

Overdue bills. Everyone has them. By the dozens. Or wait, maybe that's just us. In any case, bills not paid by the 10th day after receipt prompt a visit from the green-clad Repo

Man. The moment he arrives on the scene, both Buy and Build modes are disabled, so you can't quickly hock items and pay the bills: it's too late, man. There's nothing you can do.

The Repo Man sucks the most valuable object in the house into his Fantastic Asimov 2000 miniaturization gun to cover the bill amount. If necessary, he'll take multiple objects to equal the value of the bill—starting with the most expensive.

> **NOTE**
>
> Here's an amusing way to avoid paying bills. If your Sim is using an object as the Repo Man repossesses it, you get the money back for the object as if you'd sold it. It requires some vigilance, though. Just keep track of what you owe. (Click on the bill pile to see the amount, but don't pay them.)
>
> Immediately after a bill explodes (signifying its overdue status), switch to Buy mode and click the Hand Tool on every object. Find the object with the value closest to (but more than) your bills. Then, use that object over and over as the Repo Man arrives and repossesses it. Note: The Repo Man usually stands still at first and waits for you to finish. Just use the object again; he'll come grab it, and you'll get your refund.

Services

Sim families have an extremely efficient network of services available to them. Firefighter, Police Officer, Maid, Repairman, Gardener, Newspaper and Pizza Deliverers—all are quite competent in *The Sims*. We highly recommend you take advantage of these services, regardless of your means.

Each service has a daily work-hour limit. Service providers work until they finish the job, unless the time exceeds the work-hour limit. When they finish their work, they flash the day's charge over their heads and leave. That amount is deducted from your household account automatically.

Not Enough Funds

If you don't have enough money in your account to pay a day's service fee, the service provider calls you a deadbeat (which, let's face it, you are) and procures household objects until their combined value equals the fee. This is only the case for the gardner, maid, and repairman. Like the Repo Man, service providers use the objects' current depreciated value, not the purchase price, and they start with objects they have already fixed.

Newspaper Delivery

The *Sim News* arrives automatically, delivered daily near the mailbox between 8:45 and 9 a.m. by your spunky paper-kid (at no charge at that!). Every midnight, that day's paper turns to trash. If five newspapers pile up in the front lawn, delivery is suspended until you "recycle" (toss out) at least one of the old papers.

> NOTE
> If a house goes back on the market (that is, you evict a family or everyone in the household dies), all hired services are discontinued. If you want services for a new family, you must hire them again.

Sims can use or read the newspaper as many times as they want before it turns to trash at midnight. But the paper features only one job offer per day. The same job offer will appear again and again if you keep looking there for a job on the same day.

Fig. 7-7. Extra! Extra! Get your SIM NEWS, delivered daily to your front walk.

Pizza Delivery

Pizza delivery is a 24-hour service. At §40 a pop, it's kind of pricey. When Freddy the Pizza Dude arrives, he won't hand over the pie if you can't pay. If you have sufficient funds, Freddy waits at the door until your Sim greets him and takes the pizza box. If no one answers the door within an hour, he'll leave.

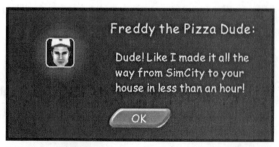

Freddy the Pizza Dude:

Dude! Like I made it all the way from SimCity to your house in less than an hour!

OK

Fig. 7-8. Freddy can deliver a §40 pizza in under an hour.

Gardener

When hired, your friendly gardening service sends a highly qualified Gardener every three days. Work hours: 9 a.m. to 6 p.m. Your Gardener waters all flowers, inside and out, and stays as long as necessary (until quitting time) to finish the work. Hourly Rate: §10. Two interactions are possible with the Gardener: Dismiss means you send the Gardener home for the day; Fire means you discontinue the gardening service.

Fig. 7-9. Watering your own flowers can take a LOT of time out of your day. The Gardener keeps your flowers alive for a mere §10 an hour and she waters in half the time a Sim takes.

Fig. 7-10. Maids are worth every penny they charge. Their thorough work lets you pile more personality points on fun, friendly traits like Outgoing and Nice.

Maid

When you hire a Maid, she works every day. This woman not only looks good, she's a cleaning dynamo. The Maid makes unmade beds, washes dirty plates, picks up and takes out trash, and cleans anything that can be cleaned—sinks, tubs, showers, toilets, mops up floor puddles, you name it. Hourly Rate: §10. Work hours: 10 a.m. to 5 p.m. And she stays as long as it takes (until quitting time) to finish the work.

Two interactions are possible with the Maid: Dismiss means you send her home for the day; Fire means you discontinue the cleaning service.

Tips from the Testers

Sims don't need to be neat as long as they have a Maid, and for just §10 an hour, she's a major bargain. Even with a house full of disgusting slobs, the most she can cost you is §70 a day. Try this: When creating a new family, don't give any points to the Neat personality trait. Just hire a maid on Day One and forget about cleaning up.

—Andrew Blomquist, Tester

Repairman

When you call for repair help, your local service sends the Amazing Mr. Fixit. This guy repairs anything—TV, dishwasher, sink, shower, espresso machine, computer, pinball machine—*any* object that can break. In fact, if you have zero mechanical Skill and a broken TV, you have no choice but to call the repair man—it's the only way to fix it. He'll even unclog toilets and replace light bulbs. Hourly rate: $50—kind of steep, but with his super-high Mechanical skill, he rarely needs to stay more than an hour. If you're suddenly running low on funds, you can Dismiss the Repairman before he finishes his work.

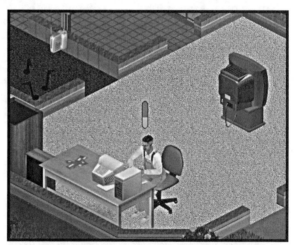

Fig. 7-11. The Repairman works fast, saving you lots of time. His computer repair skills are impeccable, but pricey (costing §100 or more).

Tips from the Testers

If time is short and you have low Mechanical skill, use the Repairman. He's not outrageously expensive—compared to the costly wasted time of repairing stuff yourself, anyway—and he works fast.

—Peter Trice, Tester

Fire, Theft, and Accidents

You know the saying: "Crap happens." Life's *not* a bowl of cherries. And, darn it, we never promised you a rose garden, either. When you hit bumps in the road, both little and big, just remember: keep a stiff upper lip. And keep the following tips in mind.

Floods

No, the riverbanks won't overflow. But *The Sims'* manual labels "flood" any spills or leaks caused by sloppy Sims or accidents—broken appliances, bladder failure, and so forth. Naturally, Room score drops if a Sim must slog through puddles in, say, the kitchen.

When messy people get out of the tub or shower, or clean the aquarium, often they leave a puddle of water on one tile of the room. This puddle can grow, but only if there's further activity. For example, if a messy person steps out of a shower where a one-tile puddle already exists, it becomes a two-tile puddle. And so on. Bladder failure also leaves a one-tile flood. Any Sim denied access to bathroom facilities can suffer this monumental indignity.

Floods created by appliance breakdowns are bigger, multitile spills. The puddle keeps growing as long as Sims keep using the source of the spill (say, a broken dishwasher) before it's repaired or removed. If you don't clean it up, a multitile spill evaporates after two Sim days.

> **NOTE**
> When directed to clean up one "flood tile" (one grid square of a spill), Sims will continue to mop up *all* flooded tiles in the room unless interrupted by another command or if their Mood score drops below zero.

Fig. 7-12. Big floods mean appliance failure. Fix the broken item quickly, or risk more flooding and rock-bottom Room scores.

Fire

Only three types of objects can cause a fire in *The Sims*—fireplaces, stoves, and the Wild Bill THX-451 barbecue. Stoves and barbecues catch fire when unskilled cooks try to cook a meal. Fireplaces don't catch fire, but their sparks can set nearby objects ablaze. (Fire can't start on a floor tile.)

Fire spreads quickly to flammable objects (including people) on adjacent tiles, so get them under control fast. Fires also can spread to empty tiles, but the probability is less. While a fire burns, Buy and Build mode are disabled. Fires awaken any Sims sleeping in the same room.

Cooking Fires

Again, cooking fires can begin on a stovetop used by low-skilled cooks. Microwave ovens can't start fires, but chances are greatest that your Toaster oven will flame up. A Sim's chance of starting a cooking fire relates to skill value, thus:

COOKING SKILL POINTS	PERCENT CHANCE OF FIRE
0	15
1	5
2	1
3–10	0

Fig. 7-13. Poolside barbecues are fun, but that nearby plant and chair are poorly placed firetraps. Keep objects off tiles adjacent to barbecues and fireplaces.

Fireplace Fires

Be careful around fireplaces! If you build one, place no furniture or other objects on tiles adjacent to it. Fireplace fires break out only when objects are right next to a lit fireplace.

Panic and Extinguishing Fires

When a fire breaks out, the Panic interaction pushes to the front of everyone's queue. Unfortunately, Sims continue to panic as long as the fire burns; they won't pick any other interaction autonomously. Thus, Sims won't extinguish fires until you order the screaming fools to do so.

In *The Sims,* each tile of a multitile blaze is considered an individual fire. Sims extinguish fires one tile at a time. When ordered to extinguish a fire, a Sim continues to extinguish individual outbreaks of the fire in adjacent tiles until no more fires remain. Careful! The Sim with the extinguisher can catch fire, too.

Fig. 7-14. Fire immediately sends Panic to the front of every nearby Sim's interaction queue. If you don't order someone to extinguish the flames, no one will!

While extinguishing a fire, a Sim's Hygiene score drops precipitously to a limit of -50. If the Sim's Energy is less than zero, it will climb to a limit of 0. This prevents Sims from falling asleep right after the arduous task of putting out a fire…and really makes them want to bathe afterward.

Fire Damage

Flammable objects burn for approximately 75 seconds before turning into an ash pile. If a fire is extinguished before the object has turned to ash, the object is unharmed. As you might expect, Sims who catch fire go much quicker. If you don't extinguish a burning Sim within a few seconds, he or she becomes a lovely, well-crafted burial urn.

Tips from the Testers

Smoke alarms are cheap! Unless all your Sims have a Cooking skill of 4 or higher, you need a smoke alarm on the wall near your stove. If a fire starts in the kitchen, the Fire Department arrives automatically.

—Syruss Flyte, Tester

Calling the Fire Department

Your local Firefighter puts out fires faster than family members, and stays until the job's done. But don't make frivolous calls. If you call the Fire Department when no fire is burning, you get a lecture and a §100 fine.

Burglars

Burglars strike randomly when a house is empty or if everyone is asleep. They steal objects, starting with the most expensive, pilfering up to five objects in a session. Your best defense: buy a burglar alarm for each room of your house as soon as you can! Buy and Build modes are disabled during a burglary, so you can't just purchase a burglar alarm when the fiend appears, or quickly sell off objects to keep them safe.

Fig. 7-15. Firefighters are skilled at (believe it or not) fighting fires. Smoke alarms in the kitchen bring them running at the first sign of a blaze.

When your alarm sounds, the Police arrive on the scene quickly. (You can try to call the Police if you don't have an alarm, but the cop rarely arrives in time.) If the

PRIMA'S OFFICIAL STRATEGY GUIDE

Police Officer arrives while the burglar is
still on the premises, the cop almost always
catches his or her man. The cop also confis-
cates stolen items as evidence. But not only
do you get simoleans from your insurance
company to replace the stolen goods (based
on their depreciated value when stolen), but
you also get a §1,000 cash reward. Sweet!

Be aware that if you call the Police when
no burglar is in house, the cop scolds you
about false alarms. Unlike false fire alarms,
however, this transgression carries no fine.
Cops, apparently, are more forgiving.

Fig. 7-16. Cops catch crooks regularly only if you make
burglar alarms priority purchases.

Tips from the Testers

The best place for a burglar alarm is
next to the portals where Sims enter
and exit the lots. Placing burglar
alarms indoors can be iffy, because
once the burglar starts running, the
cop can't catch him. Placing alarms on
a wall segment at lot corners will alert
the Police the moment the burglar
steps into the lot; cops will catch the
burglar every time, and give you §1,000
for the catch.

Fig. 7-17. Tips for the Truly Paranoid: Install burglar
alarms on single wall panels at lot corners. Detect
thieves before they even reach the house!

And here's another tip. Two Sims
can corral the burglar until the cops
arrive. Have one Sim call the Police and direct the other to stand on the tile
next to the front door. The burglar will route to the back door (if there is
one). Now hustle and stand on the tile next to the back door. (Slow the burglar
by keeping your cursor over him.) The burglar will route back to the front
door. Repeat until the Police Officer shows up. If you have only one door, you
can still slow the burglar by trying to get in the way, but the cad will get
through eventually.

—Andrew Blomquist, Tester

8
Building

Building a dwelling can (and should) be a highly creative act of personal expression. This is particularly true when the builder has access to the kinds of tools you find in *The Sims*. So we hesitate to offer you "strategies" for constructing your own dreams (or nightmares). Who knows better how to do that than you?

Of course, we can offer some simple, common sense sort of guidelines. This section reiterates many of the Quick Tips embedded in *The Sims* in-game Help System. We also pass along a few fun tips from those twisted EA testers. But, in general, our advice is *go for it*. That's the real beauty of Will Wright's philosophy of game design. His goal: put the creative tools in your hands and let *you* be the game designer.

Fig. 8-1. Remodel existing homes or build from scratch on an empty lot. Either way, THE SIMS construction tools are easy to use.

NOTE

Visit www.thesims.com regularly to download more floor patterns and wall textures for your construction and remodeling projects or get tools for creating your own.

Tips from the Testers

Resist the urge to build too big. In a huge home, your Sims waste far too much time just walking around. The best tactic for expanding your house is to increase the size of your rooms incrementally (adding better windows, wallpaper, floors, and furnishings) only until the Room score is maxed out. This way you have all of the benefits of a large house, but your Sims won't have to spend half an hour walking from the fridge to the table.

—Andrew Blomquist, Tester

A Special Note on Remodeling

Before we discuss building options, let's reiterate an important point we made in the previous section about *un*building options. One of the great joys of *The Sims* is the ease with which you can remodel existing homes. Tear out a wall here, add floor space there, scrape off that ugly Hollywood Hills mauve stucco and replace it with something elegant, rip up old, cheap carpeting and lay down some gorgeous hardwood or gray shale flooring. What a blast!

In the rush to remodel, however, players sometimes forget that their old walls and floors are worth simoleans. Yes, materials depreciate over time, but their value never drops below 80 percent of their initial cost. (See "Build Depreciation" in the "Sim Economics" section.) However, if you just cover over existing tiles, the old stuff just disappears, *poof,* no cash back.

The point: *always delete used floor and wall coverings as the first step in remodeling!* This sells the old stuff back and adds funds to your remodeling budget.

Fig. 8-2. If you decide to remodel, be sure to strip off old wall and floor coverings (interior and exterior) for the depreciated cash refund before putting on the new stuff.

TIP

Always remove old paint or wallpaper before repainting a room to get some of your original investment back. Do the same with floor tiles: delete old tiles before placing new ones.

Architecture Items

What follows is a quick review of some Build mode basics.

Undo/Redo Items

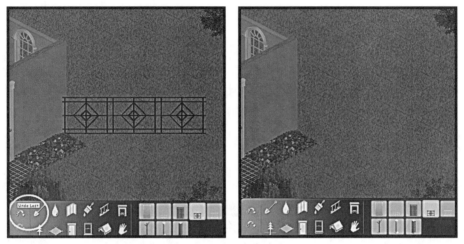

Fig. 8-3. Oops. That diagonal balustrade looks pretty stupid. Just hit the Undo button to wipe it from your design slate.

Mistakes happen. Hey, even Frank Lloyd Wright had regrets. Too bad he didn't have an Undo button. During any building session you can click the Undo icon to reverse the last change you made (and get *all* your money back). Keep clicking it to undo previous changes. Once you leave Build mode, however, your changes become permanent. After that, you can delete them, but you'll lose some money to depreciation.

Selling Items

If it's too late for Undo, you can get money back for most architectural items by deleting or selling them. Things you can pick up you can delete using the Hand tool. Other architectural tools have more specific instructions. Click a selection's thumbnail under each tool to learn how to delete it.

Fig. 8-4. When in doubt about how to place or delete any architectural item, just click on its thumbnail to get directions (and a full description of the item).

Rotating/Moving Items

You can use the Hand tool to delete, move, or rotate many architectural items, free of charge.

Terrain Tools

Hills are interesting. Dales aren't bad, either. Or maybe you *want* a boggy, mosquito-breeding trench ringing your property. *The Sims* terrain tools let you raise and lower earth with abandon. And the way-cool "water_tool" cheat gives you additional landscaping options.

Here's a look at the basics of terrain adjustment.

Level

You need level ground for most objects and all Sim-to-Sim interactions. To create flat ground, click on the Level Terrain tool, and then click-and-drag out a rectangle. The land in the rectangle becomes the same height as the spot where you first clicked the mouse. Grass will grow back by itself over time.

Fig. 8-5. The Level Terrain Tool

Hilly

As you probably deduced, the Raise Terrain tool raises terrain. Just click or click-and-drag to raise terrain level. But here's a little tip. If you hold down Ctrl as you raise terrain, the tool goes nuts and you can make some nice curvy hills.

Fig. 8-6. The Raise Terrain Tool

The Water Tool Cheat

We told you about this cheat earlier in "Cheats and Quick Start Tips," but we mention it again here because…well, because it's just so darn neat. Press [Ctrl][Shift][C] to bring up the Cheat window, and then type in water_tool. Now you can add dramatic ponds, quiet creeks, sibilant streams, or wet, festering peat bogs to your property. Just remember, your Sims can't route through water.

Fig. 8-7. We routed this lovely meandering stream past our brownstone cottage, adding some indigenous greenery to create a peaceful garden setting. (Then we applied for writing jobs at landscaping magazines.)

Plant Tool

Landscaping the grounds is so easy, we have little to say about the tool itself. Just click to place plants, flowers, and trees where you want them. Move or delete them with the Hand tool. That's it. But keep the following, very helpful tips in mind.

Effect of Outdoor Plants on Room Score

Outdoor plants raise your Sims' appreciation of an area and thus improve their Room scores. Remember, everything outdoors on the lot is considered one big room. EA tester Andrew Blomquist says, "The outside Room score is very important, because Sims are always outside before they go to work. Make sure you build a lot of room for your Sims and plant lots of trees."

Fellow tester Syruss Flyte agrees, adding, "Put plenty of flowers, shrubs, a fountain, and so forth in the yard. As Sims walk to the car pool, they'll get a big Room score boost. This helps raise their mood and, hence, their job performance rating."

But, of course, if flowers or flowering bushes aren't cared for, they'll die. If your Sims don't have time to look after flowering plants, prepare to spend money on a Gardener.

Flower Care

Flowers start as buds. They follow a three-day cycle: if you don't water them, they wilt in three days, and die in three more. Dead flowers, of course, will push your Sims' Room scores in the negative direction. Note that you can water wilted flowers before they die. Watering wilted flowers is free and thus much less expensive than replacing a patch of dead flowers with a new purchase.

When you direct a Sim to water a patch of outdoor flowers, he or she will continue watering *all* outdoor flowers unless you insert another command in the queue, or until the Sim's mood falls below -50.

By the way, stomping on blooming flowers makes them wilt; if they've wilted already, or haven't yet bloomed, a good stomping kills them dead. Note the Sims only stomp autonomously if their mood is low. You cannot direct them to do it.

Plant Trees for Ease

Yes, you must water flowers regularly. Trees and shrubs, however, require no mainte-nance: they never wilt or die, yet they add roughly the same to your Room score as flowers do. So tree-planting is a good way to boost outside Room score without the expense of hiring a Gardener or spending precious time watering plants yourself. Of course, trees are more expensive than flowers.

Wall Tool

Walls are kind of important to a house. They hold up the roof, among other things. In *The Sims,* they also become the crux of the privacy issue.

The Privacy Issue

Consider two things when you design your room layout. First, Sims need privacy to perform bath-room functions. If other Sims are in the bathroom, a Sim won't bathe or use the toilet, regardless of Bladder or Hygiene scores. (To Sims, bladder accidents are preferable to being seen using a toilet. Go figure.) Second, Sims can't sleep if noisy objects such as TVs, stereos, pinball machines, computers, or exercise machines are being used in the same room. So your bedroom best be enclosed.

Fig. 8-8. Bathroom privacy is a design issue you can't escape, no matter how modern you feel. Bedrooms should be enclosed space, as well, to avoid unwanted wake-ups.

Tips from the Testers

When playing with large families, bathroom privacy can be a problem. Build multiple small bathrooms to avoid having your household Sims interrupt each other's bladder and hygiene functions. One bigger bathroom with a shower or bath is fine; then add a couple of extra two-by-one-tile toilet-only rooms. These work really well, and are relatively inexpensive.

—Syruss Flyte, Tester

Drag Out Rooms

Here's just a little reminder. You can build a complete room in one fell swoop by holding down [Shift] as you drag out a wall. Keep [Shift] pressed until you release the mouse button.

Removing Walls

To delete a wall, hold down [Ctrl]. The wall cursor changes to a wrecking ball. Then draw over the existing wall to remove it. Be sure to hold [Ctrl] down until you've released the mouse button.

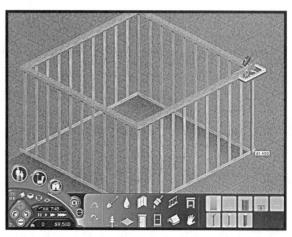

Fig. 8-9. Shift-click and drag out walls to create entire rooms in one smooth motion.

Diagonal Walls

Sims like roomy rooms with lots of corners. The more corners, the better. So slice the corners off rectangular spaces with diagonal wall sections. (See Figure 8-10.) Diagonal walls can make the house look a little nicer, too. Don't overdo it, though. You can't place doors, windows, or objects on or against diagonal walls.

TIP

Make it easier for your Sims to navigate through the house by leaving at least two grid squares between walls.

Fig. 8-10. The bay window nook in this house-in-progress not only looks nice, but its diagonal walls add more corners to the room, boosting your Sim's Room score.

TIP

Sims like big rooms. And the more corners the better.

Columns

You can place columns with the Wall tool, as well. Using columns as support, you can build a second-story deck or, our favorite, a catwalk connecting stone turrets ringing the perimeter of our "compound." (We've always wanted a compound.) Each column supports a 3-by-3-tile floor area, so a second-floor deck can extend five tiles out.

Floor Tool

You don't have to waste time placing one floor tile at a time. Click-and-drag to place a rectangle of tiles, or hold down [Shift] and click to cover the whole room at once. The reverse is true, too. To remove a rectangle of tiles, hold down [Ctrl] and then click-and-drag. To remove an entire room's flooring, hold down [Shift][Ctrl], and then click on any tile in the room.

When removing a rectangle of tiles, be sure to release the mouse button *before* you release [Ctrl]. If you reverse that order (releasing [Ctrl] first, mouse button second), the floor tool will place the selected tile pattern on the rectangle you've dragged out instead of removing the existing floor tiles.

> **CAUTION**
>
> Sims become quite displeased with unfinished rooms, as you might expect. If you overspend on wall space and don't leave enough funds for wall or floor coverings, watch that Room score plummet! Of course, it's also good to note that Sims have no preference for wall or floor coverings—they just care that they are covered.

Wallpaper Tool

You don't have to place wall covering one strip at a time. You can paint or wallpaper a whole room by holding down [Shift] and clicking the left mouse button. Holding down [Shift] is also a nice way to preview how the room's walls will look with the selected covering.

To remove a wall's paint or wallpaper, hold down [Ctrl] while using the Wallpaper tool. To clear a whole room, hold down [Ctrl][Shift], and then click the Wallpaper tool on the wall.

Doors and Windows
Door Tool

Doors are one of life's unsung essentials. They let you come and go, of course. But in *The Sims,* most doors can provide light, too. Along with increasing a room's size, light is one of the best ways to improve a Sims' feeling about a room—that is, raise their Room motive scores.

Don't waste money on installing doors unless the room is totally enclosed. Sims won't use a door if there's any other access to a room. If a room isn't enclosed, don't enclose it with objects. Even if there is a door, your Sims will not enter the room.

TIP

Doors are a single tile wide. To create lovely double doors, place them side by side and rotate them using the < > keys.

How to Delete Doors

To delete doors, select the Door tool and hold down ⌃Ctrl. The cursor becomes the Delete icon (a circle with slash through it). Move the Delete icon over the door you want to remove. When that door is highlighted, click to remove it.

A deleted door is replaced by a section of wall covered by the paint or wallpaper on the surrounding wall. Note that you also can remove a door by using the Wall tool to draw a wall over it. The result is the same as if you removed it using the Delete icon.

Fig. 8-11. Doors are more than just access portals in THE SIMS. Paned models like the Monticello add necessary light to a room, too.

Window Tool

Sims like rooms with lots of light. The bigger the room, the more windows it takes to brighten it during the day. Note that all windows give the same amount of light whether large or small.

How to Delete Windows

To delete windows, select the Window tool and hold down ⌃Ctrl. The cursor becomes the Delete icon. Move the Delete icon over the window you want to remove. When that window is highlighted, click to remove it.

A deleted window is replaced by a section of wall covered by the paint or wallpaper decorating the surrounding wall tile. You also can remove a window by using the Wall tool to draw a wall over it. The result is the same as if you removed it using the Delete icon.

Water Tool (Swimming Pool)

Swimming in a pool improves your Sim's Fun score, and it has the side benefit of improving Body skill. Sims can use the pool ladder to Get In or the diving board to Dive In. Exit is impossible without a ladder, however. As mentioned, swimming builds Body skill points, but not as quickly as working out on the Exerto exercise machine. Also, swimming doesn't follow the usual skill development rules; for example, a Sim needn't be in a good mood to swim.

Tips from the Testers

If you're feeling sadistic, or just want to get rid of those annoying visiting Sims, build a swimming pool moat all the way around your house. On the resulting "island," put ladders into the pool, and on the outside edge of the pool put only a diving board.

When unsuspecting neighbors come over to visit, they dive into the pool and

Fig. 8-12. We tried Syruss Flyte's perverse "human trap" moat. It worked beautifully, man. Here we see four neighbors starving in the pool/moat.

climb out onto the island. When these visitors leave, they climb back into the pool, but have no way to get back out—except to return to *Death Island*. Eventually, trapped neighbors die of starvation. You can acquire an impressive cemetery on your lawn this way.

—Syruss Flyte, Tester

Fig. 8-13. And here we see the final results—six gravestones. And no more solicitors.

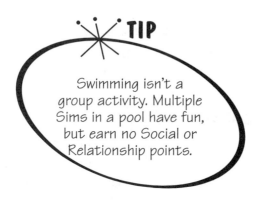

TIP

Swimming isn't a group activity. Multiple Sims in a pool have fun, but earn no Social or Relationship points.

Stairs

Stairs connect the first story to the second. When placing stairs, they automatically cut a hole in the second floor. You can place stairs outside, as well, to connect to balconies; just make sure they connect to a floor tile on the second story.

Second Story

The transparent grid on the second story represents tiles the first-story construction supports. These are the only areas on the second story where you can place floor tiles and walls. Use columns to extend this area, if you like.

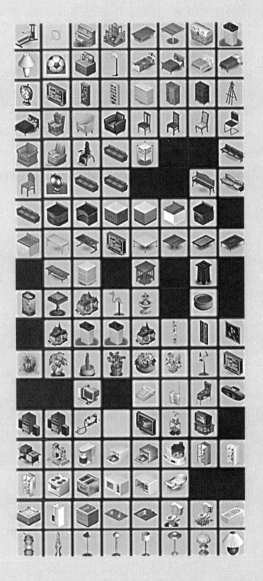

9
Sim
Objects

Here it is—the big honking section you've been waiting for. Objects! Dozens of them! Lined up in neat catalog rows, all there for the taking—if you have the simoleans, that is.

NOTE

Visit *www.thesims.com* regularly to download more catalog items.

We open with some notes about how Sim objects are appraised, repaired, sold, moved, and so on. Then we provide an exhaustive rundown of the game's catalog items and other objects, in alphabetical order. Use it as a handy, A-to-Z Sims shopping guide.

How Sims Appraise New Purchases

Sims can be snobs. Each new item bought and placed in a Sim household broadcasts a Come and See Me message. Sim residents respond by examining the object and expressing a response—positive (clap), negative ("uh-uh" and a red X through the object), or indifferent (shrug). The quality of the stuff they already own modifies this response. The more expensive their current stuff, the less likely they are to find new stuff very exciting.

See? Snobbery.

Here's how it works. Sim response to new objects relates to the average value of all objects in the household. The game takes the following steps:

Fig. 9-1. This fellow likes his new computer desk. Reaction to a new object is based on a formula that compares its value to the average value of a Sim's other stuff. The more expensive the new item, the more likely the Sim is to approve of the purchase.

- Calculates the average value for all objects in the household.
- Subtracts 10 percent of the new object's value for each copy of the same object that exists. (Sims don't get as excited about the third large-screen TV as they did for the first.)
- Compares values.
- If the new object's value is more than 20 percent above the average value for all objects, your Sim claps a positive response.

- If the new object is less than 20 percent below the average value for all objects, your Sim waves a negative response.

- If the new object is between 20 percent above or below the average value for all objects, your Sim shrugs an indifferent response.

Repairing Broken Objects

When something breaks, a Sim can either fix the item or call the neighborhood Repair service. Even Sims with zero Mechanical points can repair a broken object; low and high skill levels are equally effective at repair. But repairs by low-skill Sims take much, much longer. If you have the cash, call a Repairman. Spend the time you save doing something more productive. Napping, for instance.

> **TIP**
>
> The game "remembers" the amount of repair work done on a broken item. If a Sim spends time repairing an object and gets interrupted, the object will need less repair time when any Sim returns to finish the job.

Buy Mode

Ah, Buy mode. It sounds so American, doesn't it? Here's where you indulge your acquisitive nature, loading up on consumer goods without leaving the comfort of your computer nook.

The Object Catalog

Online catalogs are fun, aren't they? Easy to use, easy to go broke. The one in *The Sims* is no different. To see a larger version of each catalog item, click its thumbnail. You'll also get a description and a rating of the object's usefulness.

Objects may be grouped for viewing by function or by room. Click the Buy Mode button or press F2 to toggle between them.

Fig. 9-2. You may group catalog items by function or by room.

Function is the default grouping. This is probably the easiest way to find objects after you've furnished a home. But when you move into a new place, it's probably easier to group objects by room. As you fill each empty room, it's convenient to view the catalog items for that room only.

Rotating/Moving Objects

After your catalog buying spree, it's easy to rearrange household objects. To move an object, click on it once (the tiles beneath highlight yellow), drag it to a new location, and click again to put it down. To rotate an object, click and hold down the mouse button as you drag it where you want.

Selling Objects

To sell an object, click on it once, and then either drag it back to the Control Panel or press [Delete]. If you sell the object back before midnight on the day it is bought, you'll get all your money back. After you've had an object for a while, its value goes down. Certain objects may increase in value over time. (For more on object depreciation and appreciation, see "Sim Economics.")

List of Object Interactions

The object types in the following list appear in the original shipping version of *The Sims*. Each description includes this useful information when it applies:

- Cost (in simoleans)
- Motives affected by interaction
- Group activity offered
- Breakable/unbreakable
- Adult-only/kid-only
- How object works and/or how best to interact with it

Pay particular attention to the motives each object affects. In general (but not always), the more expensive an object, the more points it boosts the affected motive. For example, expensive chairs are more comfortable; expensive computers are more fun.

Alarm: Burglar (§250)

Goes off when a burglar enters the room. Calls police automatically. Keeps blaring until burglar leaves the room. Wakes up sleeping adults and kids in the same room. When placed on the exterior of a house, it detects outside burglar motion within five grid tiles. For more about burglars, see Fire, Theft, and Accidents in the Sim Economics 101 section.

Alarm: Smoke (§50)

Goes off if a fire starts in the same room. Calls Fire Department automatically. Continues ringing until fire is out. Wakes up Sims sleeping in the same room. For more about fire, see Fire, Theft, and Accidents in the Sim Economics 101 section.

Aquarium (§200)

Motives: Fun. Tank gets dirty if not cleaned. Fish die if not fed. Fish die quicker in a dirty tank. There's no cost to feed the fish but it does cost to restock them. Boosts Room score.

Ash Pile

An ash pile appears on the floor after fire destroys an object. Ashes drag down Room score. Can be swept up.

Baby

Motive: Fun (if you choose Play). Yes, babies are "objects" in *The Sims.* Fun objects. Sometimes. For more on babies, see Family and Housemates in the Social Interaction section.

Bar (§800)

Motives: Fun, Hunger, Bladder (lowers). Adult can have a single drink or make multiple drinks for a group of adults; drinks don't cost money. Kids don't make drinks, but can open the bar fridge and take out a can of soda.

Barbecue (§350)

Motive: Hunger. Adults only. Grilling food creates a group meal platter. Can start a fire if a burnable object sits on an adjacent tile, but the BBQ itself won't burn. For more about fire, see Fire, Theft, and Accidents in the Sim Economics 101 section.

Basketball Hoop (§650)

Motives: Fun, Energy (lowers). Group activity. One or two people can play at once. Family member can play alone. Visitors must join a family member to play. (For more on joinable activities, see Keeping Visitors Happy in the Social Interaction section.) Higher Body skill increases chances of making a basket. Max Fun available varies according to Active trait rating.

Beds (§300–§3,000)

Motives: Energy, Comfort. Five models available. Once a bed has been slept in, it appears unmade. Unmade beds lower Room scores. Note that more expensive beds fill your Energy needs faster, saving you about an hour of sleep per night. They are also more comfortable. For more on beds, see Sleeping with Housemates on page 92 and Energy on page 35.

Bills

These arrive in the mailbox every three days. Sims must pay their bills within 10 days or the Repo Man comes and repossesses household items. Color-coded:

- White: Not overdue
- Yellow: Three days overdue
- Orange: Six days overdue
- Red: Nine days overdue

For more about bills, see Bills and the Repo Man in the Sim Economics 101 section.

Bookshelves (§250–§900)

Motive: Fun (for Read, not for Study). Improves Cooking and Repair skills. Three models available. Read Books, Study Cooking or Mechanical, Study for School (kids only). Sim goes to nearest vacant chair and sits to read. If chair is unavailable, Sim reads standing up. Sims must be directed to study. However, Sims (particularly Serious ones) will read a book on their own to raise their Fun scores. All bookshelves give Skill points at the same rate. For more on skill-building activities, see the Careers and Skills section.

Chairs: Movable (§80–§1,200)

Motive: Comfort. Six models available. Sit to relax or engage in seated activity—Watch TV, Play Chess, Eat, Use Computer. Sims may seat themselves from the back and scoot the chair forward to a desk or table.

Chair: Plush (§80–§500)

Motive: Comfort. Four models available. High Comfort. Sims can't scoot plush chairs to tables or desks. More exensive chairs provide more Comfort.

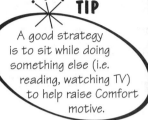

✳ **TIP**

A good strategy is to sit while doing something else (i.e. reading, watching TV) to help raise Comfort motive.

Chair: Recliner (§250–§850)

Motive: Comfort, Energy (Nap). Two models available.

Chessboard (§500)

Motive: Fun. Group activity. Improves Logic skill. (For more on skill-building activities, see the Careers and Skills section.) One person can play alone or with a second person. (For more on joinable activities, see Keeping Visitors Happy in the Social Interaction section.) Max Fun point value varies by personality. Serious types have more fun. But Sims won't get bored if Fun levels are maxed out, because they can play for Logic skill. For more on this, see the Mood and Motives section.

Clock: Alarm (§30)

Once set, it rings two hours before car pool arrives for any sleeping Sim in the room. (If the Sim is awake, the alarm won't sound.) However, it awakens everyone in the room regardless of car-pool time. Once set, it functions daily until unset.

Clock: Grandfather (§3,500)

Motive: Room. Adults only. Once wound, runs for 24 hours. When it runs down, it advertises high Room points until it's wound again.

Coffee: Espresso Machine (§450)

Motives: Energy, Fun, Bladder (lowers). Adults only. Drink Espresso. Affords a greater energy boost than regular coffeemaker. Breaks down randomly.

Coffeemaker (§85)

Motives: Energy, Bladder (lowers). Adults only. Less energy boost than espresso machine.

Computers (§999–§6,500)

Motive: Fun. Four models available. Play Games, Get a Job, or Study (kids only). Breaks based on use. The cheaper the computer, the sooner it breaks. (Just like real life!) Only three jobs available each Sim day. Playing computer games awakens sleeping adults in the same room (but not kids).

Counters (§150–§800 per section)

Five models are available—four kitchen, one bathroom. Food Prep, Serving Group Meals, Object Placement. Not an Eating Surface!

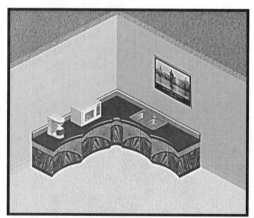

Fig. 9-3. Counters can round off corners nicely. To create a corner section, place a regular counter at a junction between counters.

You may not sell or delete a counter if something sits on it. But if you move the counter, anything on it moves with it.

You may place and use bathroom counters in the kitchen, and kitchen counters in the bathroom. If the kitchen has no counter or food processor, your Sims may use a bathroom counter to prepare food. Counters add Food points, and you need them to prepare most meals. The trick is to keep Sims from leaving things on them! For more on food, see Hunger: The Food Chain Revealed, in the Mood and Motives section.

Desks (§80–§800)

Three models are available. Used primarily to place objects such as computers, lamps, telephones, and the like. Desks are listed as "desk/table" in the catalog, and can be used as Eating and Serving surfaces. In fact, if you're tight on space, use a desk instead of a table. They fit easier into snug spaces. No Food Prep, though; only counters work for that.

Dishwasher (§550–§950)

Breakable! Using the dishwasher is faster than washing dishes in the sink. Placement or Serving Surface, but not Eating Surface. Random breakdowns—cheaper model breaks more often. Floods if used after it's broken.

Dollhouse (§180)

Motive: Fun. Group activity. First person to play always goes to the open side of the dollhouse. Max Fun points varies according to Playful personality rating. For more on joinable activities, see Keeping Visitors Happy in the Social Interaction section.

Dresser/Armoire (§250–§1,200)

Four models—two dressers, two armoires. Change Clothes. Units never run out of clothes. Adults and kids can use it to change into PJs, swimsuit, or regular clothes. Adults also can change into formal wear or work clothes. Sims can change out of their default clothing using the dresser/armoire, and even change their body type, adding or losing 100 pounds.

Easel (Painting) (§3,500)

Motive: Fun. Improves Creativity skill (adults only).

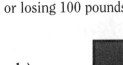

(For more on skill-building activities, see the Careers and Skills section.) More than one Sim (one at a time) can work on a painting to completion. A completed painting may be sold. Its value depends on an average of skills of those who painted during its cycle: skill 0 = §0; 5 = §25; 10 = §500. Sims in a bad mood won't paint. For more on this, see the Mood and Motives section.

> **NOTE**
> In general, characters won't choose to develop skills autonomously. The easel and piano are exceptions. They're Fun objects, as well; that is, using them raises a Sim's Fun score.

Exercise Machine (§700)

Motive: Energy (lowers). Improves Body skill. (For more on skill-building activities, see the Careers and Skills section.) When used, awakens all Sims sleeping in the same room.

Fireplaces (§600–§3,000)

Light a Fire. May be placed anywhere (inside or outside) against a wall. Fireplace burns for two hours and always adds to Room score, but more so while lit. Anything combustible in an adjacent tile will catch fire, but not right away.

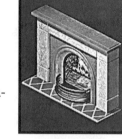

> **NOTE**
> Technically, fireplaces are placed in Build mode with the Fireplace tool, not purchased from the Buy mode catalog.

Flamingo (§12)

Motive: Fun. May be viewed or, better, kicked. Increases Room score, so it's not totally useless. Quite a bargain at a mere §12.

Food Processor (§220)

Motive: Hunger. Food Prep. Adds more Hunger points to the meal than using a counter; faster, too. Preparer's Cooking skill affects Food Prep duration. For more on food, see Hunger: The Food Chain Revealed, in the Mood and Motives section.

Fountain (§700)

Motives: Fun, Bladder (lowers). Can Play with fountain. Sims who are Shy (low Outgoing) like the fountain most. Adds to Room score.

Flowers: Gift

Friends bring flowers periodically, handing them over during greeting. Increases Room score. Gift flowers wilt in two days.

Hot Tub (§6,500)

Motives: Comfort, Fun, Hygiene. Group activity. Breakable. Adults only. Get In, Soak, Talk, Have Fun. If the first person in has Outgoing 7 or above, he or she gets in naked; otherwise, the Sim wears a swimsuit. Joiners follow the first person's example. Sims can have regular conversations as they soak, and won't get out until all hot tub motives are maxed or a motive falls very low. For more on joinable activities, see Keeping Visitors Happy in the Social Interaction section.

Fig. 9-4. Hot tubs are pricey, but worth it. They satisfy four needs—Comfort, Fun, Hygiene, and (if other Sims join) Social.

Lamps (§25–§350)

Breakable (bulb burns out). Seven models—three floor, four desk. Lights turn on automatically when the first Sim enters the room, and turn off when the last Sim exits. You can turn lights on and off manually, which overrides the automatic system until 8 a.m. the next day. Anyone can replace a bulb, and it costs nothing; the time it takes, however, depends on Mechanical skill, and there's a random chance of electrocution. (Repairman never gets electrocuted.)

Lamp: Garden (§80)

Exterior ground placement. Lights turn on automatically at 6 p.m. and off at 2 a.m. They don't break.

Lava Lamp (§80)

Motive: Fun. Adds small amount to Room score. Doesn't break.

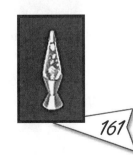

Medicine Cabinet (§125)

Motive: Hygiene. Improves Charisma skill (adults only). Brush Teeth to raise Hygiene. For more on skill-building activities, see the Careers and Skills section.

Mirrors (§100)

Two models—one wall, floor. **Improves Charisma skill (adults only).** For more on skill-building activities, see the Careers and Skills section.

Newspaper (Free!)

Motive: Fun. Read for a small amount of fun, or Look for a Job. Delivered daily; once there are five papers on the property, delivery will stop until one of them is recycled. Offers only one job per day, and as with the computer, Sims in a bad mood won't look for jobs.

Painting (§45–§7,600)

Motive: Fun. Seven choices. (Our personal favorite: "Snails with Icicles in Nose.") Boosts Room score. The more expensive, the more points it contributes. Serious Sims get the most Fun. Sim attitude toward certain paintings is predetermined: the same person always likes or dislikes the same painting, even if it's in a neighbor's house. It's not a function of personality, mood, or anything else.

> **NOTE**
> Painting and sculpture value appreciates and depreciates randomly.

Phone (§50–§75)

Motives: Fun, Energy (lowers). Call neighbors or services; answer for various reasons. See Calling Neighbors in the Social Interaction section. Phone rings if:

1. Chance-card call offers proposition, always for money. Example: "You just won §100 on KSIM." No calls at night.

2. Prank phone call. Example: "Do you have Prince Albert in a can?"

3. Boss calls to warn Sim about missed work.

4. A Sim has lost their job.

5. Friends are being ignored.

6. Offers the adoption of a child.

Piano (§3,500)

Motives: Fun. Improves Creativity skill. (For more on skill-building activities, see the Careers and Skills section.) Quality of sound (the actual music) improves as skill increases. If the player has high Creativity skill, the watcher gains Fun and Relationship points toward the player. Watchers offer negative response if a player has low Creativity. Visitors play only if their Creativity is 8 or higher. (For more on joinable activities, see Keeping Visitors Happy in the Social Interaction section.) When played, a piano can awaken sleeping adults (not kids) in the same room. If a Sim kid is playing, the Sim adults will be nice and give a positive response—no matter how good or bad the performance is.

Pinball Machine (§1,800)

Motive: Fun. Group activity. Breakable. Gives a nice Fun boost, but Playful Sims have more fun. Visitor can join only if family member is playing already. (For more on joinable activities, see Keeping Visitors Happy in the Social Interaction section.) Two players take turns. When played, awakens sleeping adults (not kids) in the same room.

Play Structure (§1,200)

Motive: Fun. Group activity. A great way to keep Sim kids happy and playing together. Max Fun points increased for Active kids. For more on joinable activities, see Keeping Visitors Happy in the Social Interaction section.

Pool (§75 per tile)

Motive: Fun, Energy. Improves Body skill. Needs ladder to exit. For more on skill-building activities, see the Careers and Skills section.

Pool: Diving Board (§300)

Motive: Fun. Best way to enter the pool.

Pool: Ladder (§200)

The only way to exit a pool, a ladder is a must-have.

Pool Table (§100)

Motive: Fun. Group activity. High Fun boost for one or two Sims. Sim pool players complete one game, and then stop (unless you order them away). For more joinable activities, see Keeping Visitors Happy in the Social Interaction section.

Refrigerator (§600–§2,500)

Motive: Hunger. Three models available. Make or Serve Meals, Get Snacks. Launches Food Prep sequence. The type of meal Sims make will depend on what other cooking appliances are available. For more on food, see Hunger: The Food Chain Revealed, in the Mood and Motives section.

Sculpture (§875–§12,648)

Motive: Fun. Four choices. (Our personal favorite: "Large Black Slab.") Boosts Room score. The more expensive, the more points it contributes. Serious Sims get the most Fun. Sim attitude toward each sculpture is predetermined: the same person always likes or dislikes the same sculpture. Sculpture value appreciates and depreciates randomly.

Shower (§650)

Motive: Hygiene. Breakable. Gets dirty. It's still usable when it's broken, but the flooded tiles increase. Before disrobing, a Sim will check to see if anyone else is in the room. If so, the Sim determines whether he or she is in love with the person. If all is clear or if the Sim is in love, he or she disrobes and enters the shower. Otherwise, the Sim tries to shoo interlopers away. After a few seconds, if not alone, the Sim will abort the shower. Messy Sims leave puddles when they get out. Neat Sims will get more Hygiene points than Messy Sims. Neat Sims also shower longer.

Sink (§250–§500)

Motive: Hygiene. Breakable. Three models available. Wash Dishes, Wash Hands. Must be placed in counters (except bathroom pedestal sink). Washing dishes at the sink takes longer than using the dishwasher. If there's no kitchen sink or dishwasher, Sims may wash dishes at a bathroom sink. Neat Sims wash hands automatically after eating pizza or using the toilet if there is a sink available.

Sofa/Loveseat (§150–§1,450)

Motives: Comfort, Energy (Nap). Five loveseats, seven sofas, one garden bench available. Sit or Nap. (Can't nap on garden bench.) Expensive sofas add to Room score.

Stereo (§100–§2,550)

Motive: Fun. Group activity (Dance). Two stereo models and a boom box available. Turn On for music; Dance Alone or with Partner. (Kids always dance alone.) Expense contributes to fun. When it's on, it awakens sleeping adults in the same room (but not kids). Outgoing Sims dance first. Shy Sims are less likely to Join Dance. (For more on joinable activities, see Keeping Visitors Happy in the Social Interaction section.) One particularly cool feature of the stereo is that you can change the songs played on it by dragging and dropping actual MP3 files into the Music/Stations/ directory.

> **NOTE**
> With each Sim who comes to dance, the lure of the stereo grows stronger. If many Sims are in the household, a dancing crowd often forms in the room with the stereo.

> **NOTE**
> For details on cooking appliances, see the "The Food Chain Revealed" section in "Sim Needs and Motives.")

Stove (§100–§1,000)

Two range-top models, two small ovens. Sims use stoves to cook prepared meals, but only after you direct them to the refrigerator. Can start fires, depending on user's Cooking skill. Microwave doesn't start fires. Toaster oven more likely to flame than other stoves. (See the "Fire, Theft, and Accident" section in "Sim Economics.") For more on food, see Hunger: The Food Chain Revealed, in the Mood and Motives section.

Table: End (§40–§300)

Seven models (including kids' nightstand) available. Place Objects, Serving Surface, but not Food Prep or Eating. Expensive models boost Room score.

Toilet (§300–§1,200)

Motive: *Bladder!* Also lowers Hygiene. Gets dirty. Expensive model boosts Comfort. Breakable (gets clogged). Two models available. Use to you-know-what. Neat Sims are more likely to flush after use. If Bladder score drops below -95, Sims run to the toilet. Clogging is based on how much was deposited since last flush. Anyone can unclog the toilet, but Sims with high repair skill do it more quickly. Expensive toilets never clog because they automatically flush. They also add to the Room score.

Tombstone/Urn

Motive: Social (lowers). Shows up automatically after a Sim dies. Can't be purchased, but may be moved or sold. If a Sim dies outdoors or an urn is moved outdoors, it appears as a tombstone. (Tombstone must be on level ground.) If a Sim dies indoors or a tombstone is moved indoors, it appears as an urn. Each midnight, there's a small probability that an urn or tombstone will generate a Sim ghost. When an urn or tombstone is sold, it no longer generates a ghost.

> **NOTE**
> Mourn lowers the Social motive score; Sims will seek other Sims for consolation. Don't be surprised if sometimes this consolation comes in strange forms (i.e. a joke or tickle). Sims have no concept of social appropriateness.

A tombstone/urn advertises the Mourn interaction very highly during the first 24 Sim-hours after a death, so family Sims will grieve autonomously at the burial site. The lure decreases over the next 48 hours. Visitors may mourn during the first 72 hours, too. After that, family Sims can mourn, but only if you direct them to do so. For more on death, see the Mood and Motives section.

Toy Box (§54)

Motive: Fun. Kids only. Play with the toys it contains for a Fun boost. Only one kid at a time can interact with toy box, picking a random toy each time—car, doll, plane, teddy bear.

Train Set: Large (§955)

Motive: Fun. Group activity. Up to 10 Sims can participate! (For more on joinable activities, see Keeping Visitors Happy in the Social Interaction section.) One Sim runs the train from the control station. Other Sims grow attracted and come to watch. The more Sims observers gather, the stronger the interaction advertises, drawing even more Sims. This continues until the controller satisfies his or her Fun motive. Then the group disbands. Also boosts Room score.

Train Set: Small (§80)

Motive: Fun. Group activity. Kids only. For more on joinable activities, see Keeping Visitors Happy in the Social Interaction section.

Trash Can: Inside (§30)

> **NOTE**
> A full trash can has a negative depreciated value: that is, it detracts from your net worth, Room score, and costs you money if you just delete it.

Throw trash or ash piles into this small, lined can. It fills up after about five deposits. Then you must empty it before you can use it again. (It fills faster than a trash compactor.) Flies appear when the can is full for six hours.

Trash Can: Outside

Comes with the lot. This can is a bottomless pit. You can't fill it up. You can't move or delete it unless you use the "map_edit on" cheat to unlock the floor tile it sits on, and then use the "move_objects on" cheat. (See "Cheats and Quick Start Tips.")

Trash Compactor (§375)

When full, its drawer opens and the green light turns red. When you select Empty Trash, your Sim pulls out the compactor's bag and takes it to the outside trash can. Serves as Placement, Food Prep, or Serving Surface, but not an Eating Surface. Holds four times as much trash as the indoor trash can.

Trash Pile

When full, has a negative impact on Room score. Appears when trash-bearing Sims find the indoor trash can full or unavailable, or when Messy Sims toss down used snack containers. Clean Up to pick up the pile (it becomes a trash bag) and dump it in nearest trash can.

Tub (§800–§3,200)

Motives: Hygiene, Comfort. Three models available. Sims soak until they get maximum Hygiene score. It gets dirty based on use. Messy people leave a puddle from time to time.

TV (§85–§3,500)

Motive: Fun. Group activity. Breakable. Three models available. Breaks with use, not age. If on, it awakens sleeping adults in the same room (but not kids). Three things modify TV enjoyment:

1. Expensive models provide higher Fun value.

2. Lazy people get more Fun points from watching.

3. Personality types get more Fun points from their preferred channels. Preferences are:
   - Outgoing: Romance
   - Active: Action
   - Playful: Cartoon
   - Grouchy (low Nice): Horror

A Sim may get electrocuted when attempting to repair a broken TV. It depends on Mechanical skill:

TV REPAIR HAZARD

MECHANICAL SKILL POINTS	PERCENT CHANCE OF ELECTROCUTION
0	100
1	25
2	10
3–10	1

VR Glasses (§2,300)

Motive: Fun. Select Play to wear. Big fun! Only one person at a time may use this. Playful Sims get the most Fun points.

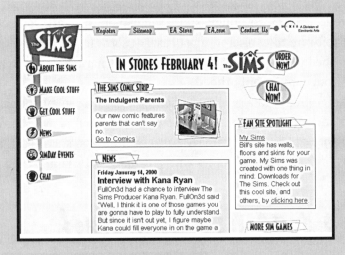

10

How to Find and Create New Sim Stuff

One of the coolest things about *The Sims* is the way you can customize walls, floors, roofs, faces, "skins" (i.e. body textures, including clothes), and even the game's music to reflect your own unique style. You can do the work yourself, using a set of Maxis-created software tools and, in most cases, a software paint program. Or you can download the finished work of others. Either way, it's remarkably easy to put a personal design stamp on your Sim Neighborhood.

This final chapter gives you a quick overview of how you can customize Sims stuff and trade it with other players. First, we'll show you how to find everything you need. Then we'll take a look at the three primary customization tools: FaceLift, HomeCrafter, and SimShow. Note that each tool comes with a detailed tutorial that you can view with your browser.

Where to Find New Sim Stuff

You can find all kinds of user-created Sim skins, faces, walls, and floors on the Internet. But your first stop for new Sim paraphernalia should always be the official EA/Maxis website for *The Sims,* located at *http://www.thesims.com.*

There you'll find plenty of official info about the game, plus links to other Sims-related sites. Look for new Maxis-created objects (see the Slot Machine in figure 10-12) and check out The Sims Exchange, a library where you can upload your Sim folks, houses, and family albums, and download the same from other players.

Fig. 10-1. Check the official Maxis website for updates, new objects, and links to other fun sites devoted to THE SIMS.

You can also find many fan sites devoted to *The Sims* on the Internet. One of the best as of this writing is Steve Bonham's "The Sims Resource" at *http://sims.xtremesimz.com.* Two other good ones are "My Sims" at *http://mysims.bizland.com* and "Mall of The Sims" at *http://www.synchroplay.com/mallofthesims.*

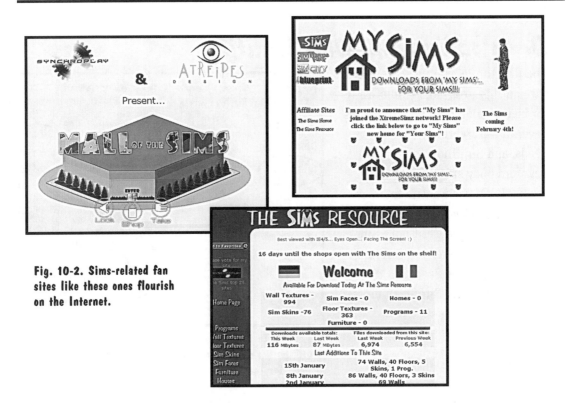

Fig. 10-2. Sims-related fan sites like these ones flourish on the Internet.

Keep in mind that Internet sites are often fluid entities. By the time you read this, the ones we've listed here may no longer exist. But trust us, you can find *lots* of good stuff out there. Even the laziest search engine should locate dozens (if not hundreds) of sites.

Where to Put New Sim Stuff

Once you create or download a new object, skin, or texture file, you must put it in the proper game folder before you can use it in *The Sims*. Here's where to save new stuff:

- Head and body textures in The Sims\GameData\Skins
- Floors in The Sims\GameData\Floors
- Walls in The Sims\GameData\Walls
- Roofs in The Sims\GameData\Roofs

How to Add New Stuff: Getting Started

Before you can start customizing *The Sims* into your own personal playground, you need tools. Fortunately, these tools are easy to find and pop into your virtual tool belt.

Downloading THE SIMS Utilities

The first things you need are the three utility programs HomeCrafter for viewing new wall and floor tiles, FaceLift for creating new Sim heads, and SimShow for viewing new Sim body skins. Go to the official EA/Maxis website for *The Sims* at *http://www.thesims.com*. Then click on the Get Cool Stuff button. From there, you can find and download the FaceLift, HomeCrafter, and SimShow tools.

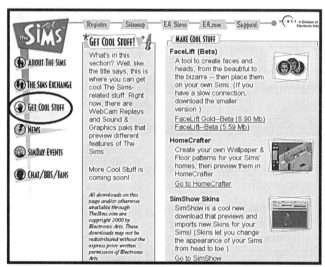

Fig. 10-3. To find customization tools, click the "Get Cool Stuff" button on the main screen of the official EA/Maxis website for The Sims.

The Difference Between Mesh and Skin

Before we go any further, let's discuss the difference between "mesh" and "skin." A skin is the colorful surface texture of a Sim—the face, skin, hair, and clothes. This texture is applied or "wrapped" around a mesh. Each mesh is a full 3D shape, body and/or head, underneath the skin—a kind of blank wire-frame space that the skin gets layered over.

You cannot edit body meshes with any Sim tool. In fact, both SimShow and HomeCrafter are merely preview tools that let you view skin or wall/floor textures previously created or edited with a software paint program. However, you *can* change head shapes and create new mesh/skin combinations with the awesome FaceLift tool. In FaceLift

Fig. 10-4. A "skin" is the colored texture that wraps around a "mesh," or body/head shape. Here's the body skin of a Sim female in shorts next to the head skin of a Sim female brunette.

you're creating actual head/face files; in HomeCrafter and SimShow, you're only viewing files previously created by either you or someone else.

All three tools let you export the files directly into *The Sims* for use in the game.

FaceLift

This tool is a blast! Accessible for all users, FaceLift allows you to design new heads for characters in *The Sims* by morphing the shape and skin of preset heads. Warning: Making heads can be addictive! This free utility is so fun and easy-to-use, you'll spend hours making your Sims movie stars and freaks.

You'll begin with nine randomly-generated heads. Choose the head that is closest to the one you want. You can now specify how different or similar to that head you want the next set of

Fig. 10-5. The FaceLift Tool

heads to be. For example, you can focus on changing hairstyle while leaving the face the same. Or, you can focus on skin color while leaving the shape of the head alone. Once you've gotten close to what you're going for, tweak the face with FaceLift's Fine Tune feature and give it a description, gender, age, and skin color. Once you've finished, FaceLift lets you export the new head directly into your game folder with the appropriate filename code. And don't worry if you don't like the finished product—you can get a new set of nine heads any time you like!

Fig. 10-6. FaceLift tools let you "fine tune" the eye, nose, and mouth/jaw areas of each face. Here's the same face twice—one with all features set narrow, the other with all set wide.

HomeCrafter

HomeCrafter allows you to preview floor and wall patterns to see how they will look in the game, then export them directly into *The Sims*. Note that this utility doesn't help you create the patterns. Instead, it loads existing images and converts them for use in the game.

So to create your own custom floor/wall tiles, start by using a software paint program (*Photoshop* or *Paint Shop Pro* are good examples) to create patterns and save them as *.bmp* or *.jpg* files. Or, if art isn't your thing,

Fig. 10-7. The HomeCrafter Tool

you can use images created by anyone or anything. HomeCrafter can load any *.bmp* or *.jpg* image file in your system, even photo image files. Imagine wallpapering a haunted Sim house with repeating images of Britney Spears. What a chilling thought! For the best results, make your images the size specified in the tutorial. Otherwise, the game will stretch them to suit its needs.

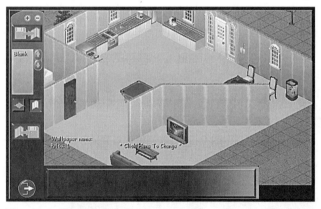

Fig. 10-8. The HomeCrafter screen consists of a control panel, a sample room to preview your custom wall/floor tiles, and the text description box on the bottom.

TIP

Here's a mini-cheat. Use HomeCrafter to save big on decorating costs. Both wall and floor tiles can be priced at as low as §1 and then imported into the game. This lets you install coverings at a fraction of the normal cost.

Once you have the .bmp or .jpg images, load them into HomeCrafter (which automatically converts the images into either wall or floor tiles) and place them in the sample room. You can enter descriptions that actually appear in the game, and set the price per tile, as well. Finally, you can export them directly into *The Sims*. HomeCrafter automatically places wall/floor tiles in the correct game folder with necessary game info.

SimShow

SimShow lets you preview new Sim body/head skins and export them into your game. As with HomeCrafter, you don't actually create files in SimShow. Instead, you view existing Sims— that is, Sims with skin textures applied to mesh bodies. The skins, however, may be ones you've edited with an external paint program (like Photoshop or Paint Shop Pro). Thus, SimShow gives you a way to preview your work. Or the skins you view may be downloaded from a friend or fan site.

> **NOTE**
> Refer back to figure 10-4 to see the kinds of body and head textures you can edit and then view on Sims to create new skins for your game.

In any case, SimShow is a fabulous viewing tool. And once you see a Sim you like, whether created by you or by someone else, SimShow lets you easily put the creation into *The Sims* by automatically exporting the images to the appropriate in-game folders and formats. The new Sim then becomes available in the game's Create a Sim screen.

Fig. 10-9. SimShow lets you view Sim characters and their animations both before and after you edit their textures.

> **NOTE**
> Getting a skin to wrap properly around a "mesh" (3D body shape) can be tricky. To learn more about editing skins, consult Maxis Assistant Producer Sean Baity's guide, included when you download SimShow. You'll get a kick out of the detailed, step-by-step tutorial in which Baity puts his own face and clothes on a Sim body shape. You can also find an excellent tutorial entitled "Skinning 101" and a skin database in the Simz Online website at http://simz.gamenation.com/features/skinning.

Other Drop-In Assets

The Sims also lets you drop your own music into the game.

MP3 Music Files

You can add MP3-format music files into game folders to personalize the music that plays in the background or on the in-game stereos. Note: You can't change the names of the in-game radio stations, just what music plays when you select a station.

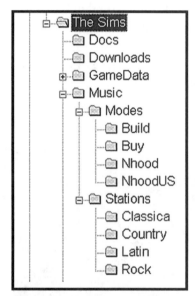

Here's where to place MP3s so they play on the station you want:

- Put Country station music in the Music\Stations\Country directory.

- Put Classical station music in the Music\Stations\Classica directory.

- Put Latin station music in the Music\Stations\ Latin directory.

- Put Rock station music in the Music\Stations\ Rock directory.

- Put Build Mode background music in the Music\Modes\Build directory.

- Put Buy Mode background music in the Music\Modes\Buy directory.

- Put Neighborhood background music in the Music\Modes\NhoodUS directory (in the U.S.—elsewhere, use the Nhood directory).

Fig. 10-10. Put your own MP3 files into the appropriate folders within the THE SIMS Music directory to get new music to play in the background or on the in-game radio stations.

Roof Patterns

You can add new roof textures to *The Sims,* too. First, create and save a pattern as a 256-color .BMP file, 32-by-32 pixels in size with a pixel depth of 8. Then drop the file into the Gamedata\Roofs folder (see Fig. 10-11).

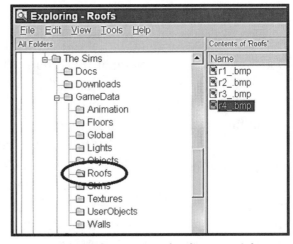

Put your .BMP roof patterns in this directory. Make sure they're the right size and pixel depth.

Objects

Over time, Maxis will release more objects for your downloading pleasure. To get them, simply go to the official website. Each new object will include auto-installers that automatically put all the files associated with the object into the appropriate directories. The first new object (available 2/4/2000) was a slot machine. Objects to follow include a moosehead, a pet guinea pig in a cage, and wall sconces.

Fig. 10-12. The first new object download available at THE SIMS official website was the venerable slot machine. Hey, what's a home without one?

> NOTE
>
> The downloadable slot machine is a money cheat. If your Fun motive is low, your odds of winning simoleans are very high!

177

Sharing Families

As *The Sims* manual points out, if you've checked the Export HTML option in the Play Options for the game, important JPEG shots of family members (w/statistics), family houses and house information is saved (by house address) in the Web Pages folder of *The Sims* directory. It happens automatically—you can just delete them if they're unwanted or edit them in an image-editing program.

This awesome web publishing tool lets you post each Sim family's web page online in The Sims Exchange and to look for other families to download into your neighborhood. To find the Sims Exchange, go to *www.thesims.com*. Then have a blast finding and downloading other people's houses. Your in-game photo album is posted online for other users to read, too. With the photo captions, it's like creating a storybook. Build your family stories day to day, then share them with others. To view your own family's web page, click the View with Web Pages button on the game's neighborhood screen.

A

Active personality trait, 14, 17, 23
ad attenuation, 52-53, 56-71
ad modifiers, 48-50
adult conversations/interactions, 75, 77, 78-79, 83
advertising
  attenuation, 52-53, 56-71
  defined, 47
  false, 48
  modifiers, 48-50
alarm clock, 36, 157
alarms, smoke/burglar, 137-138, 155
Animation Preview mode, 5
anti-aliasing, 174
appliances, 25-27, 111, 134, 168. See also specific appliances.
aquarium, 155
armoire, 159
art, 34, 123, 162
ash pile, 155
attacking, 82-83, 85
attenuation, ad, 52-53, 56-71
autonomy
  cheat code, 3
  and interaction queue, 46-47
  of visitors, 101

B

babies, 92-94, 155. See also kids.
Backrub interaction, 82, 85, 89
balloons, routing, 5
bar, 155
barbecue, 27, 155
basketball hoop, 156
bathing, 33, 164
bathrooms, 145, 158, 162, 164

beds, 156
bill-paying, 129-131, 156
Bladder motive/score, 23, 33, 41, 145
Blomquist, Andrew, iv
.bmp files, 173, 175
Body skill, 17, 149
Bonham, Steve, 170
bookshelves, 112, 156
bubble_tweak cheat, 3
Build items/actions, 129
Build mode
  selling/deleting items, 129, 142
  tools, 140, 143-150
  and Undo button, 128, 142
building tools, 140, 143-150
burglar alarm, 137-138, 155
bus, school, 118
Business career track, 104
Buy mode catalog, 23, 38, 152, 153-154

C

candy, 31
car pool, 109-110
career tracks
  choosing, 104-105
  list of, 104
  and skill-building, 104, 105, 110-112
  table of benefits/requirements, 112-117
catalog, Buy mode, 23, 38, 152, 153-154
chairs, 156-157
chance cards, 110
Charisma skill, 17
cheat codes, 2-6
chessboard, 157
children. See kids.
cleaning service, 133
clocks, 36, 157

clothes, 128
coffee, 157-158
color bars, motive, 20
columns, support, 147, 150
Come and See Me message, 152
Comfort motive, 23, 32-33
computer, 105, 158
construction, building, 140, 143-150
contribution curves, happiness, 50-52
conversation
    how it works, 77-78
    scoring, 78
    topics/icons, 75-77
Cooking skill, 25, 26, 27, 112, 137
corners, room, 37, 146
counters, kitchen/bath, 25, 27, 30-31, 158
Creativity skill, 17
Crime career track, 104
customizing tools, 171

D

death, 42, 101-102, 166
decay
    motive, 23, 109
    relationship, 73-74
depreciation
    build, 128-129, 141
    object, 122-127
design team, v, 2
desk, 158
difficulty, food, 24
DirectX 6, 171
dishwasher, 159
diving board, 163
dollhouse, 159
Door tool, 148

draw_all_frames cheat, 3
draw_floorable cheat, 3
draw_routes cheat, 3
dresser, 159

E

easel, 159
Easter egg, 2
economics, 121
electrocution, 43, 111, 168
Electronic Arts, v
employment, 7-8. See also career tracks.
Energy motive, 23, 35-36, 41, 137
Entertainment career track, 104
espresso machine, 157
exercise machine, 159
exit conditions, 53-56
exporting faces/textures, 175, 179

F

FaceLift utility, 171, 176-179
faces, customizing, 176-179
failure states, motive, 41-44
false advertising, 48
families, 91, 121
Family Friend Count, 88
family history cheat, 4
file names, texture, 181-182
fire, 43, 112, 135-137, 159
fired, getting, 108, 109, 133
Firefighter, 137
fireplace, 37, 129, 136, 160
flamingo, 160
Flirt interaction, 82, 83, 86, 89
flood, 135
floor covering, 129, 141, 147, 172-175

Floor tool, 147
floorable cheat, 3
flowers, 129, 144-145, 160
.flr files, 175
Flyte, Syruss, iv
food
    cleaning up, 32, 38
    cost of, 28
    difficulty values, 24
    and Hunger motive, 24, 27, 44
    preparing, 25-27, 30-31
    types of, 28-31
food processor, 25, 27, 160
fountain, 160
frames cheat, 3
Freddy the Pizza Dude, 24, 132
Free Will, 46
friendship, 73, 88-89
fruitcake, 31, 32
Fun activities, 55
Fun motive
    and happiness contribution value, 51
    and kids, 35, 95
    and personality traits, 16-17, 34, 49
    and TV channels, 34
furniture, 32-33, 156-157, 159, 164

G

game manual, v, 73
games, saving, 7
Gardener, 132, 144
genable cheat, 4
ghosts, 101-102
gift foods, 31
God, 46
grades, Report Card, 118-119
grandfather clock, 157

grass cheat, 4
grid cheat, 4
Grill interaction, 27
Grouchy personality trait, 16, 17
Group Meal, 28, 30-31
Group Talk, 74, 79-81, 82
grow_grass cheat, 4

H

hair style/color, customizing, 176-179
Hand tool, 142-143, 144
happiness contribution value, 50-52
history cheat, 4
HomeCrafter utility, 171, 172-175
hot tub, 13, 33, 55, 81, 160-161
house
    construction/remodeling tools, 140
    maintenance of, 37, 54
    size considerations, 140
    two-story, 150
housemates, 91-92
Hug interaction, 82, 86, 89
Hunger motive. See also food.
    decay/failure, 23, 41, 44
    and food, 24, 27, 28, 44
    and happiness contribution value, 51
    points, 28
Hunger points, 28
Hygiene motive/score, 33, 137

I

icons, conversation, 75-77
interactions
    canceling, 46
    exit conditions, 53-56
    and object types, 56-71, 154-168
    priority, 47

interactions, continued
    queue, 46, 48, 53
    romantic, 89
    social, 73
interests cheat, 3, 75

J

jealousy, 82
job levels/requirements, tables of, 112-117
job performance, 106-108
jobs, 7-8, 107-108, 112-117.
    See also career tracks.
.jpg files, 173

K

kids
    and conversation topics, 75-77, 78-79
    and Fun motive, 35, 95
    and personality traits, 15
    and school, 112, 118-119
    and social interactions, 83, 95
    and tax credits, 94
Kiss interaction, 74, 82, 83, 88, 89
kitchen, 158
klapaucius cheat, 2

L

lamps, 161
landscaping, 144-145
Law Enforcement career track, 104, 109
Lazy personality trait, 14, 23
Level Terrain tool, 143
levels, job, 113-117
Life of Crime career track, 104
lighting, room, 37
locking, tile, 4

log, game, 5
love, 74, 89
loveseat, 164

M

Maid, 133
maintenance, household, 37, 54
Maintenance skill, 112
Make Cool Stuff button, 171
"Mall of The Sims" website, 170
manual, game, v, 73
map_edit cheat, 4
marriage, 8-9, 90-91, 121
Max [Motive] factor, 17, 23, 34, 55
Maxis, v, 140, 170, 171, 182
meals, 28. See also food.
Mechanical skill, 43, 111, 112, 134
medicine cabinet, 162
Medicine career track, 104
Messy personality trait, 12
microwave, 26, 27
Military career track, 104, 108, 109
Military School, 119
mirrors, 162
money
    and bill-paying, 129-132, 156
    cheats, 2, 6-7
    conversation icons, 75
    for kids, 118
Mood, calculating, 20-22
Mood bars, 20-21
Morales, Jason, iv
motive decay, 23, 109
Motive Engine, 20-21
motive failure states, 41-44
motives, 20, 23, 154. See also specific motives.
mourning, 166

move_objects cheat, 4
music, 34, 165
"My Sims" website, 170

N

Neat personality trait, 12, 134
needs, basic, 20, 23
Neighborhood God, 46
neighbors, 95-101, 149
net worth, 122
Newbie, Bob and Betty, 6-7
newspaper, 132, 162
Nice personality trait, 16

O

Object Depreciation table, 123-127
objects. See also specific objects.
    appraising, 152-153
    billable, 130
    buying/selling, 153-154, 154
    and depreciation, 122-127
    interactions/point values, 56-71, 154-168
    positive/negative, 37, 38-41
    repairing, 153
    rotating/moving, 4, 154
O'Tey, Ed, iv
Outgoing personality trait, 13-14, 17

P

painting, 162
personality traits
    and career tracks, 105
    and Fun score, 16-17, 34, 48
    list of, 11
    and skill-building, 17
    and zodiac signs, 18
phone, 96, 98, 162

piano, 163
pinball machine, 163
pizza, 24, 28-29, 132
Pizza Dude, 24, 28-29, 132
Plant tool, 144-145
play structure, 163
Playful personality trait, 15, 17
Police, 137-138
Politics career track, 104
pool table, 163
preview_anims cheat, 5
priority interactions, 47
privacy, bathroom, 145
Pro Athlete career track, 104, 109
promotion, job, 107-108
"push" interaction, 48

Q

queue, interaction, 46, 48, 53
Quick Meal, 28, 29-30

R

Raise Terrain tool, 143
refrigerator, 24, 27, 163
Relationship score, 73-74
remodeling, home, 140-141
Repair activities, 54, 111, 153
Repairman, 134, 153
Repo Man, 130-131, 132
Report Card, 118-119
repossession, 130-131
romantic interactions, 89
Room motive, 37-41
Room Score table, 38-41
roommates, 91-92
rooms, creating, 146
rotation cheat, 5
route_balloons cheat, 5

S

saving games, 7

school, 95, 112, 118-119

Science career track, 104

sculpture, 162, 164

Serious personality trait, 15, 17

service providers, 131-134

set_hour cheat, 5

shower, 164

shrubs, 129, 144

Shy personality trait, 13-14

sim_log cheat, 5

simoleans, 121, 122, 154. See also money.

SimShow utility, 180-182

sim_speed cheat, 5

sink, 164

skill-building

    and career tracks, 104, 105, 110-112

    exiting, 54

    and personality traits, 17

skin type, customizing, 180-182

sleep, 35-36

smoke alarm, 137, 155

snacks, 28, 29

social interactions

    defined, 73

    factors affecting outcomes, 81-83, 84-85

    and personality traits, 74

scoring, 73-74, 85-88

    table of adult/child, 83

social life, improving, 81-82

Social motive, 23, 36, 73

social outcomes, 81-85

sofa, 164

speed cheat, 5

stairways, 150

starvation, 44

stereo, 165

Steve Bonham's "The Sims Resource," 170

stove, 26, 27, 165

sweep cheat, 5

swimming pool, 42, 149, 150, 163

T

table, end, 165

tables

    Adult/Child Interactions, 83

    Career Track Benefits/Requirements, 112-117

    Effect of Outcomes on Social/Relationship Scores, 85-88

    Exit Conditions, 54

    How Appliances and Surfaces Affect Hunger Score, 27

    How to Get the Career You Always Wanted, 105

    How to Improve Skills, 111

    Hunger Score for Each Meal, 28

    Object Advertising, 56-71

    Object Depreciation, 123-127

    Personality Traits and TV Channels, 34

    Room Score, 38-41

    Sim Zodiac Signs, 18

    Skills Accelerated by Personality, 17

    Social Outcome Factors, 84-85

    Traits that Raise Max Fun Value, 17

    Visitor Activities, 100-101

    Visitor Start Motives/Exit Conditions, 98-99

talking, 74, 77-80

tax credits, 94

telephone, 96, 98, 162

television, 34, 168

terrain tools, 143-144

testers, Electronics Arts, iv.
See also Tips from the Testers.

textures
body, 181-182
wall/floor, 173-175

tile_info cheat, 6

tiles, locking, 4

tips, Quick Start, 6-9

Tips from the Testers, v
building, 140, 145, 149
careers and skills, 108, 110, 112
economics, 121, 131, 134, 137, 138
mood and motives, 35, 37, 42
objects, 161
personality traits, 13, 14
social interactions, 74, 81, 91, 102

toaster oven, 26, 27

toilet, 165

tombstone, 101, 102, 166

toy box, 166

train set, 166

transportation, 109-110

trash, 32, 38, 167

trees, 129, 145

Trice, Peter, iv

tub, 167. See also hot tub.

tutorials, 6, 170

TV, 34, 168

U

Undo button, 128, 142

urn, 101, 102, 166

utility programs, 171.
See also specific programs.

V

visitors, 95-101, 149

VR glasses, 168

W

w cheat, 6

Wall tool, 145-147

wallpaper, 141, 147, 172-175

Wallpaper tool, 147

walls
and depreciation, 129
doing without, 9
privacy issues, 145
and remodeling, 141, 146, 172-175

Water tool, 149

water_tool cheat, 2, 144

webcam cheat, 6

websites
DirectX, 171
fan, 170
Maxis, v, 140, 170, 171, 182

weddings, 91

weighting, motive score, 20-22, 37

Window tool, 148-149

.wll files, 175

Wright, Will, iii, v, 2

X

Xtreme career track, 104

Z

zodiac signs, 18